Appalachian Wilderness

". . . and the first day when everything is shining, and breaking up, when across the heavy streams, from the melting snow, there is already the scent of the thawing earth; when on the bare thawed places, under the slanting sunshine, the larks are singing confidingly, and, with glad splash and roar, the torrents roll from ravine to ravine."

—*Ivan Turgenev* (A Sportsman's Sketches)

Common in rich woods below 3,500 feet, sharp-lobed hepaticas (Hepatica acutiloba) *bloom in March and April offering flowers that vary in color from white to pink to lavender.*

Eliot Porter

Appalachian Wilderness

The Great Smoky Mountains

Natural and Human History by
Edward Abbey

Epilogue by Harry M. Caudill

PRESS

Grateful acknowledgment is made for permission to quote the following:
  "After Sunset" from *Wilderness Songs* by Grace Hazard Conkling.
Copyright 1920 by Holt, Rinehart and Winston, Inc. Copyright 1948 by
Grace Hazard Conkling. Reprinted by permission of Holt, Rinehart and
Winston, Inc.
  "when faces called flowers float out of this ground." Copyright 1950
by E. E. Cummings. Reprinted from his volume *Poems 1923–1954* by per-
mission of Harcourt Brace Jovanovich, Inc.
  "Autumnal" from *Collected Poems of Rolfe Humphries,* copyright © 1965
by Indiana University Press. Reprinted by permission.

The drawings by William Bartram on pages 56 and 57 are reproduced
from *Bottanical and Zoological Drawings, 1756–1788,* © 1968 by The American
Philosophical Society.

The drawing of the Sequoia on page 64 is reproduced courtesy of The
Museum of the American Indian.
Quotatioins selected and captions written by Jack Macrae.

Published in 1988 by
Arrowood Press
A division of LDAP, Inc.
166 Fifth Avenue
New York, NY 10010

By arrangement with E.P. Dutton, 2 Park Avenue, New York, NY 10016.

Arrowood Press is a registered trademark of LDAP, Inc.

Library of Congress Catalog Card Number: 87-70942

ISBN: 0-88486-012-4

Printed in Hong Kong.

*Low mountain ravines reveal the fringed polygala
or gaywings (Polygala paucifolia) which usually
flower during late May in the Great Smokies.*

*"Far back in the eighteenth century, when this was
still Cherokee country, inhabited by no whites but
a few Indian traders, William Bartram of Philadelphia
came plant hunting into the mountains of western
North Carolina, and spread their fame to the world.
. . . It was the botanist who discovered this Eden
for us."*

—*Horace Kephart* (Our Southern Highlands)

Contents

Appalachian Wilderness

The early yellow violet, Viola rotundifolia *is the most common yellow violet in the Appalachians.*

1. Appalachian Pictures

Coming Home

Going back to the Big Smokies always reminds me of coming home. There was the town set in the cup of the green hills. In the Alleghenies. A town of trees, two-story houses, red-brick hardware stores, church steeples, the clock tower on the county courthouse, and over all the thin blue haze—partly dust, partly smoke, but mostly moisture—that veils the Appalachian world most of the time. That diaphanous veil that conceals nothing. And beyond the town were the fields, the zigzag rail fences, the old gray barns and gaunt Gothic farmhouses, the webwork of winding roads, the sulfurous creeks and the black coal mines and—scattered everywhere—the woods.

The trees. Vegetation cradle of North America. All those trees transpiring patiently through the wet and exhilarating winds of spring, through the heavy, sultry, sullen summers into the smoky autumns. Through the seasons, years, millennia. Sensitive and sensible plants, with who knows what aspirations of their own.

Through town and into the hills, I'd follow a certain road for about ten miles until I came to a church and a graveyard on top of a tall hill. (I worked there once, tending that graveyard and the dead, firing the furnace in the church on winter Sunday mornings, me the sexton, best job I ever had, all that rich grass, all that meditation, all those ghosts that haunt the human mind, all that deep dark dank earth rich in calcium, all those lonely clouds with rosy bottoms drifting pensively on the horizon for a while after sundown, inviting questions, when it was time to go home.)

Time to go home. From the top of the hill you can look down into a long emerald valley where a slow stream meanders back and forth, back and forth, in long lazy loops like somebody's intestines strewn casually over the ground, through overgrazed pastures in which cows drift along the contours of the slope as slowly as clouds. All facing in the same direction. Beyond the end of that particular valley, not in it, in the mostly woods and submarginal cornfields that lay beyond, was my home.

You go down into that valley, an easy, pleasant sort of walk, past the little farms, barns, tile springhouses, pickup trucks, hayrakes and mowing machines, until you come to a big creek—that's Crooked Creek, glowing with golden acids from the mines upstream—and across the creek and up a red-dog road under a railroad trestle through a tunnel in the woods. I call it a tunnel because the road there is so narrow and winding that the trees on either side interlace their branches overhead, forming a canopy that in winter, under the typical gray sky of winter in that country, looks like a network of fine, artistic cracks in a decaying plaster ceiling, and in spring and summer like an underwater vision of translucent algal green, and in the fall, naturally, like the scales of a fire dragon. From shady green to dying flame.

At the far end of the living tunnel, beyond it and in the open, under a shimmer of summer sun or behind a curtain of whirling snow or within a lavender mist of twilight condensing toward darkness, stood the house. An austere and ancient clapboarded farmhouse, taller than wide when seen from the road, it had filigreed porchwork, a steep-pitched roof and on the roof lightning rods pointing straight up at the sun or stars; half the year there would be smoke winding out of the chimney and amber lamps burning behind the curtains of the windows.

Slinking toward me across the damp grass would come a familiar dog, always older, always more arthritic than she was ten years before. Too timid to growl, too shy to bark, she always remembered me. Her job was to guard those doors that, in nearly thirty years, had never been locked. Nobody even knew if there was a key.

Home again. Time to slop the hogs, Paw.

That's what going back to the Big Smokies always reminded me of. That hill country in North Carolina, eastern Kentucky and eastern

---

The low-growing trailing arbutus, or Mayflower (Epigaea repens), *is found among pines and oaks in remote Southern forests. Its sweet-smelling white or pink flowers appear in March at the low altitudes. Large flowering patches of arbutus can be seen above 5,000 feet during May. The leathery leaves remain green all winter.*

Tennessee seems today something like Punxsutawney, Pennsylvania, thirty years ago. Like Seneca and Powhatan, like Home, Pa., where many of us were once brung up. All of it Appalachian, winter or summer, then and now. Land of the breathing trees, the big woods, the rainy forests.

Treat Yourself to the Best

That's what it says on the side of most any barn in these parts. "Chew Mail Pouch," it says. "Treat Yourself to the Best." That way a farmer gets at least one wall of his barn painted free, by the tobacco company. Coming down through the extreme southwest corner of Virginia into Tennessee, we saw that legend many times, as often as "Jesus Saves" and "Get Right with God."

When I saw the red claybanks, though, I knew I was in the South for sure. Land of romance and myth, of chitlin and chigger, of country-cured ham, Dr. Pepper and Colonel Sanders' Kentucky Fried Chicken, finger-lickin' good. Of good poets, too, like Newton Smith of Tuckasegee, for example, and brave good men like Harry Caudill of Letcher County. Homeland too and burial place of Thomas Wolfe. That alone justifies the existence of North Carolina.

Approaching Gatlinburg, Gateway to the Big Smokies, we drive down a highway whose shoulders are sprinkled and ditches lined with glittering aluminum litter. Immortal beer can, immutable chicken basket, eternal plastic picnic spoon. At night the round ends of the cans gleam in your headlights like the glowing eyes of foxes. The hillsides are carpeted with a layer of automobile hulks. Trentville, Tennessee, where all old cars come to die, explained a man at a filling station. Poor hillbillies buy them used in Cleveland and Detroit, get laid off and come home, abandon them when the clutch gives out, the valves burn up, the retreads peel off, the pistons freeze within the worn-out rings.

Orphans. Another thing we notice coming into the South is this: while most of the farmhouses get smaller and flimsier, a few of them get bigger and fancier. Along the road, unpainted frame shacks one story high, but here and there, now and then on a hilltop, you see a grand brick plantation house with white columns framing its entrance, the house centered in a spacious park of lawn and shrub and tree, approached by a winding asphalt drive. Power.

Comical, conical hills appear, like the hills in

Bird's-foot violets (Viola pedata) *have the largest flowers of the fifty species of violets in the southern highlands. Depending on location, these plants—with leaves like "birds' feet"—flower from April until June.*

hillbilly comic strips—Snuffy Smith, Li'l Abner— with sagging gray shacks snagged on their summits. The leafless trees of winter, looking like the bristles on a brush, stand against the skyline. In each yeoman's frontyard there is a great pile of coal. Prepared for winter. The deadly fumes of coal smoke float on the breeze. Somewhere nearby, somebody's home and farm is being disemboweled by dragline, Euclid and power shovel to provide such fuel for this person in the shack, for TVA and Oak Ridge ("sub-capital of Death"), for Con Edison, etc., for you and me. Vast crimes are being committed in this region, whole hillsides raped and robbed, life systems that required ages for their weaving ripped apart.

But it's all legal. As local boosters eagerly point out, strip mining does provide jobs as well as fuel the turbines. What would you have those men do, weave baskets? fire bricks? bake biscuits? We'll have more on this matter latter. And who, you might be thinking, is "they"? That reference-less pronoun. Nobody knows exactly who "they" are, that's part of the trouble. They is It, that's all I know, that fantastic labyrinthine sky-towering ziggurat of iron and stone, paper and wire, glass and aluminum and cement, habit and obedience through which we creep and scurry in our channeled runways, us 200 million nice, neat mice. Call it The Leaning Tower of Babel. Call it what you will, it's the greatest thing since Atlantis went down with all aboard, explosions in the boiler room and rockets firing at the moon.

We drive through fields of dead goldenrod in the gray chill air of December. Snow gleams in bald patches on the blue mountains beyond. We pass tawny hills, more ramshackle shacks and pause for a while at a deserted crossroads to contemplate an abandoned country store.

The store just sits there in the cloud-filtered daylight, its old silvery clapboards warped and sprung, shakes dangling from the edge of the roof, screendoor ajar and hanging by one rusty hinge, the long front porch sagging in the middle, the whole aching creaking vacant structure canted to the east, in line I suppose with the prevailing winds.

We read and photograph the messages placarded in tin on the walls:

Chesterfields Are Best for You
Drink Dr. Pepper
Drink Coca-Cola
Drink Nesbitt's California Orange
Take Home Kern's Bread
Try W. E. Garrett & Sons' Sweet, Mild Snuff:
A Taste Treat
Buy Merita Bread Vitamin-Enriched

"How freely one drinks in the air, how quickly the limbs move, how strong is the whole man, clasped in the fresh breath of spring!"
—Ivan Turgenev (A Sportsman's Sketches)

Failure. Capitalism sounds good in theory but look at this old store. Heartbreak and bankruptcy. The metal signs are rusting, they are loose, they flap and rattle in the wind. We pass on.

Past rocky pastures. Beautiful gray-green boulders mottled with lichen rise from, or sink into, the tough winter grass. Cows lounge about in the vicinity, picking their teeth, not getting much accomplished. Sumac and willow stand with glowing leaves and glowing skin along the fencerows. Mighty white oaks grow on the higher ground, their dried-out red leathery leaves still clinging to the stems.

Dead trees and dying trees draped in vine come into view on both sides of the road. They are victims of the creeping kudzu, *Pueraria lobata*, a parasitic vine imported from the Orient back in the late 1920's. Entire trees are enmeshed in the smothering stuff, trapped and wrapped like flies in a spiderweb. A gift, like karate and kamikaze, from Japan, this fast-growing exotic has spread over much of the Smoky Mountain area, creating expensive eradication problems both for homeowners and for the National Park Service.

More trees and different trees, a bewildering variety of trees, display themselves and we're not even in the mountains yet. Hemlock, white pine, pitch pine and other conifers, and rows of planted Scotch pine for the Christmas tree market.

Here's an ancient country church, painted white but faded to gray, with a high cupola on the roof and the bell missing. The New Era Baptist Church—like the store we had passed a mile before, this church looks derelict. Christ Was Here. Religion and the failure of capitalism. Soul food for thought. Who stole the bell? Some Baptist, probably. May he be totally immersed in Hell, that'll learn him.

Into the hills we roll on joyous wheels, into the past. Way up yonder on the mountainside hangs a real log cabin with real blue smoke coming from the chimney. Near the road we pass an old barn made of squared-off logs. But it has a sheet-metal roof, not shakes. Close by, underneath a handy pine, is a Farmall tractor, a 1940's model, rusting away. The barn is covered with vinery, but not kudzu; looks more like *Wisteria frutescens*, an attractive plant even when not in flower.

Into a little valley. Here we find farms that appear to be actually inhabited and worked. Some of the houses are painted. Some of the Chevvies are new. Some of the barns, while not nearly so grand as Pennsylvania barns, look fairly well kept up; they have gambrel roofs and overhanging eaves at one end to shield the open gable from rain; through that opening under the end of the roof hay is carried by hayfork and pulley from outside up, and into the mow.

Prosperity. High on a graded, grassy hill stands another red-brick chateau: Ole Massa's house; it makes a lovely picture from the road below with its white fluted pillars two stories high, the classic pediment, the tall windows flanked by shutters. It must be good to live in a home like that, watching the peasants toiling in the fields, junkyards and gas stations down there in the bottoms. It's got to be good living up there, otherwise what's the point of all the rest of us dying down here? If only passing through on our way to the park. (We are all merely tourists in this world. Just poor wayfaring tourists. Sextons out of work, seeking new graveyards.)

Beyond the happy valley, we enter the foothills again. More hillbilly shacks appear, with smoking chimneys and staring children. Why aren't those children in school? I ask, scenting something sociological. Because it's Saturday, says Judy. A stickler for objective fact, she'll come in handy here.

We see a stand of trees that look like a type of juniper. On closer inspection, we see that they actually *are* junipers, or what is called here eastern red cedar, *Juniperus virginiana*. There is no true cedar in the Western Hemisphere, the botanists assure us. But I'm thinking of an old song I heard somewhere:

> *You just lay there by the juniper*
> *When the moon is shining bright,*
> *And watch them jugs a-fillin'*
> *In the pale moonlight . . .*

Clair de lune. Pommes de terre. One thinks of Debussy and his big hit. Of white lightning, lead poisoning and rusty-red radiators. Shine on, harvest moon.

And then we come to the main highway.

The Failure of Capitalism

Here we are, me and Judy and Suzie, trying to get to the national park, and what happens, we have to run a gauntlet of raw capitalism.

We'd forgotten what Industrial Tourism is like. Having got lost about fifty miles ago, on purpose, staying off the Superstate Interstate so far as possible, we were happily following this narrow winding rural road that led us up hill and down dale, through farmyards and mountain meadows, through potato field, woodlot and corn patch.

We were out in the country, out there where the *people* used to live. Picnic country, good place to throw beer cans, out there among the forgotten general stores and the deconsecrated churches. Hysterical hens tearing across the path of the car, hogs rooting in the oak groves, an old horse resting his chin in the crotch of a butternut tree and watching life pass him by. We saw hand-built WPA bridges arching polluted but pretty streams where great old leprous-skinned sycamores lean above the water. We passed slightly crumpled farmhouses with swings hanging by chains on their front porches (for the old folks and for lovers), and the frontyards where threadbare auto tires hang on ropes from the boughs of sugar maples (for the kids to swing on). We saw an antique John Deere tractor, the kind with iron lugs instead of rubber on the wheels, and a flatbed Ford truck with two flat tires, and recently completed autumn plowing on the tilted hillside and cornfields with the fodder still in the shock.

Yes—scenes of melancholy beauty and bucolic melancholy, under the ivory, pearl-gray sky of December, where Jefferson's agrarian America makes its final stand. In the pastures of remembrance.

And then, following this road, at a safe and sane distance behind some reckless rustic who was tooling his Plymouth into eternity at 30 mph, we come barreling round a turn into the Knoxville-Gatlinburg highway and the mainstream of the way things are. By this I mean Sevierville, Tennessee, and the Little Pigeon River, full of filth, and the walls of billboards on either side of the pavement, busy selling something fake:

GOLDRUSH JUNCTION—Cowboys, Indians & Outlaws: Gunfights Every Day

FORT APACHE—Gunfights Hourly—Live Saloon Shows

FRONTIERLAND [illustrated with a picture of a Sioux Indian in full ceremonial regalia]—Cherokee, N.C.

Don't Miss the New WAX MUSEUM—See Alan Shepard, Sgt. York real-as-life

See GHOST TOWN, MAGGIE VALLEY, N.C.—Real Life Gun Battles!

The fringed phacelia (Phacelia fimbriata) *whitens the forest floor in April and May.*

FABULOUS FAIRYLAND—Exciting Fun Rides for All Ages

MYSTERY HILL—Amazing Force of Gravity

GHOST TOWN IN THE SKY—Realistic Indian Battles

HILLBILLY VILLAGE—Copter Rides, Flea Market, Souvenirs

CAR MUSEUM & KAMP GROUND

JUNGLE CARGO—Indian Mocassins, Ice Cold Cider, Thick Rich Malts

CHRISTUS GARDENS—Outstanding All-Year All-Weather Attraction

GATLINBURG SKY LIFT—Your Shortcut to Heavenly Delight

Oh, well, it's only innocent fun. Like any fungus. No harm in it. We proceed past the motels, filling stations, and Frigid Queen shake-and-burger joints—about ten miles of them—to the bright clean tourist town called Gatlinburg. The Gateway to the Park. Here we make camp for the night in a pleasant motel room with a wood fire burning in a genuine fireplace. (Small extra charge for use of firewood says a sneaky notice on the door.)

Tomorrow we shall conquer Clingman's Dome. By Volkswagen. Looking up from the side of the motel swimming pool—water the color of antifreeze—through the chill pellucid air, we can see the Big Smokies all covered with snow. They look like real mountains.

In the meantime, however, we make a tour of

Gatlinburg. The town looks so sharp and neat it's obvious the inhabitants take great pride in the place. The motels and hotels are big, handsome, all new and all, no doubt, comfortable. (Extra charge for firewood?) Over the course of several evenings, we sample the food in various restaurants and find it uniformly good. I'm no gourmet —my favorite meal here is country-cured ham and red-eye gravy, with yams, black-eyed peas, mashed potatoes and a pitcher of Budweiser—but I do know the difference between honest food and thawed-out ersatz, no matter how hungry I get.

Gatlinburg lies in a dry county, so I suppose some might lament the lack of legal booze. But one can learn to live without it, at least for a few days at a time. In the wintertime, the off-season, with half the public places closed, there is no entertainment of any kind, not even a movie theater, but this too is an irrelevant concern. We're here to see the Great Smokies not the films or

This is the wakerobin (Trillium erectum), *whose flowers are usually a deep red but vary to green and, in the Appalachians, to white like these. This species is variously called stinking-Benjamin or the wet-dog trillium, because of its disagreeable smell.*

cabarets. Newspapers are available, if you like to read newspapers. And there's TV IN EVERY ROOM.

Also curio shops. Gas stations. Drugstores. Laundromats. Everything the heart desires. A discreet and limited use of neon tubing. No pig-iron mills rumbling night and day and belching garbage into the air. No roar of traffic, no thunder of jets, no machine-gun rattle of air hammers in the streets. Gatlinburg, at least in winter, is as tidy and efficient and quiet and sanitary as a Swiss ski village. The blatant and vulgar commercialism of Sevierville, only a few miles back the way we came, is not in evidence here.

The Compleat Tourist Town. In the restaurants blue gas fires burning under stacks of ceramic logs that look almost real until you get close. Omnipresent in the background that bland tapioca-like sound my wife calls "department-store music." Decor by Holiday Inn—all the motel lobby furnishings, all the restaurant tables and chairs and lighting fixtures, look as though they came from the same factory somewhere in Southern California. Everything designed by a neurotic suffering from a severe case of social irrelevance.

What's the alternative to this comfortable mediocrity? A grand European-style luxury that most of us would not be able to afford? Or a return to the mode of a century ago, coming into a mountain village on horseback, having a cold supper by lamplight in the cabin-kitchen of some

morose mountaineer, while savage coon dogs howl, slaver and snarl on the other side of the door, and going to sleep in the early dark on a cornshuck mattress, prey to a host of bloodsucking vermin?

Which would you really prefer? Which would I really prefer?

You won't believe me but I'll tell you: I fancy the latter, i.e., the horse, cabin, dogs and bugs.

Thus we see the secret failure of American capitalism. For all of its obvious successes and benefits (this book, for example, is being published by Jack Macrae, a maverick capitalist friend of mine), capitalism has failed to capture our hearts. Our souls, yes, but not our hearts.

So much for political economy. Walking at night through the quiet streets of Gatlinburg—where have all the tourists gone?—I look up, above the motel-hotel rooftops, and see the dark forms of the mountains bulking beyond, snow gleaming in the starlight.

Real mountains.

The early-blooming Allegheny serviceberry or shadbush (Amelanchier laevis).

"All things belonging to the earth will never change —the leaf, the blade, the flower, the wind that cries and sleeps and wakes again, the trees whose stiff arms clash and tremble in the dark, and the dust of lovers long since buried in the earth—all things proceeding from the earth to seasons, all things that lapse and change and come again upon the earth—these things will always be the same, for they come up from the earth that never changes, they go back into the earth that lasts forever. Only the earth endures, but it endures forever."

— Thomas Wolfe (You Can't Go Home Again)

2. Appalachian Rock

The Geological Construct

According to the Hardshell Baptists who largely occupy and dominate the area, the Appalachian Highlands were formed in the year 4004 B.C. by divine fiat. For theoretical elaboration of this hypothesis, the questioner is referred to the professors and Bible-lab technicians of such schools as South Carolina's Bob Jones University —known locally as Holy Bible A&M, the buckle on the Bible Belt—where the Bible is taught without apology as being literally and fundamentally the actual word of God. The teaching of evolution is just now legal in Tennessee.

According to the Cherokee Indians, who have lived in the area much longer than the Baptists, the mountains were formed in a somewhat different manner. First, they say, all living things dwelt in the sky. There was no earth at that time but only a vast body of water, and endless ocean. As the sky became overcrowded, the people and animals there sent a water beetle down to this ocean to seek land. The beetle dived to the bottom of the ocean and brought up some mud which immediately began to grow and grow until it became what we now call the earth.

Thirteen hundred native species of flowering plants, including the fire pink (Silene virginica) *and shepherd's-cress or wild stonecrop* (Sedum ternatum), *have been identified within the Great Smoky Mountains National Park.*

While the earth lay still in a soft and plastic state, a great buzzard, grandfather of all buzzards, was sent down from heaven to dry the soft earth mud with the beating of his wings. As he flew over Cherokee country, this buzzard became very tired, sinking so close to the surface that his wings struck the soft earth and formed the ridges, mountains and valleys that later became known as Appalachia.

Now in the mythology of the geologists we have still a third version of how the mountains came to be. Here is the story which geologists teach *their* children:[1]

Once upon a time, long, long ago, more than 500 million years ago, vast quantities of muds, sands and gravels were deposited, grain by grain, on the floor of what was probably a shallow inland sea. As these sediments gradually accumulated, they formed layers more than 20,000 feet in thickness. Under the tremendous pressure of their own weight, combined with the chemical action of water that cemented the particles together, the sedimentary masses became transformed into the rocks known as the Ocoee series, after a local place name. The Great Smoky Mountains are composed largely of these rocks.

The Ocoee rocks are so old that they contain no traces of plant or animal life. There are no fossils here. Like the Archean rock of the Grand Canyon's inner gorge, the Ocoee series is Pre-Cambrian. Where did it come from? Apparently from still earlier and nameless hills or mountain ranges, for the Ocoee rock contains fragments of feldspar and quartz which appear to be derived from a former granite mass that must have existed at one time in the present vicinity of the Great Smokies. The Ocoee conglomerate resembles granite, being composed of similar materials, but is in fact a sedimentary rock formed by the breaking up, deposition and reconsolidation of the former granitic sands and gravels.

In the creation of the Great Smokies, rock-making was only the initial step. After the Ocoee sediments were laid down and petrified, a renewed period of mountain-making began.

During the Paleozoic era, about 200 million years ago, occurred what geologists call the Appalachian revolution. Powerful crustal move-

A section of the largest virgin forest in the east.

There are more varieties of trees in the Smokies than in all of Europe. Of the 130 Southern species, the yellow birch and buckeye, the eastern hemlock, the cucumber, the sourwood, the tulip and red spruce—even the late lamented American chestnut—have all reached their greatest heights in the Smokies.

[1] For this interpretation I have borrowed freely from Philip B. King and Arthur Stupka, "The Great Smoky Mountains" *Science Monthly*, 3 (1950), 31–43.

ments caused the land surface to buckle, fold and break, forming overthrust faults. The effect may be compared to that of crushing a stiff sheet of tinfoil: what was formerly level and smooth becomes wrinkled, irregular, three-dimensional, an array of ridges and valleys. (As if a great buzzard had flown too close to a plain of soft mud.) At the time of this geological disturbance, the ancient Pre-Cambrian sediments were not only tilted, folded and otherwise rearranged, but also to some extent metamorphosed by the extreme heat and compression of the process into crystalline rocks such as garnet and mica.

Geologists assure us that this wrinkling of the earth's crust should not be envisioned as a dramatic convulsion of earth and rock but rather as a slow, gradual process which consumed hundreds of thousands perhaps millions of years. In this respect the Appalachian revolution may be likened to changes believed to be taking place at the present time in the mountains along the Pacific shore or to such a phenomenon as the still-continuing elevation of the Kaibab Plateau in northern Arizona.

One result of the overthrust-faulting action was that older layers of rock—the Ocoee series—were forced not only upward but also outward, sliding in great sheets over layers of younger rock in the area. An example of this effect is revealed at Cade's Cove, where the process of erosion has revealed Ordovician limestone, of the Paleozoic era (200 million years old), overlain by masses of Ocoee rock (500 million years old). Since the Ordovician rock must have originally been deposited on top of the Ocoee, the subsequent reversal of their positions indicates the extent and power of the crustal upheaval.

How do the geologists determine that one layer of rock is older or younger than another? Obviously not simply by the observation of spatial relationships. The youngest rock, like the youngest dog, is not always on top. By what, then? Essentially through paleontology, the study of fossils, which in turn is based upon the assumption that living things, both plants and animals, have evolved through the course of time from simple to more complex forms, if not without some dips and reversals in the process. Although newer methods of clocking geological time are now being developed, based on discoveries in the physical sciences, the geologist and his students still rely chiefly on the type of knowledge and the type of inferential reasoning, elegantly refined and elaborately documented, that inspired Darwin and Wallace over a century ago. And the doctrine of evolution, in turn, depends for much of its validity upon the discoveries and assumptions of the science of geology. Evolution and geology form a circular system, interdependent, based as much on logical coherence as on correspondence to observed fact.

What do we really know? We know that the sun rises and the sun goes down (or rather that the earth's movements make it seem so), that babes are born and that men die, that water flows from the mountain tarn home to the river and sea, that autumn is followed by winter and winter by spring, that the same flower that bloomed last summer will never blossom again. These are the kinds of things we know, the only things we can take for absolute certainty. All the rest is philosophy. All the rest is mystery.

I do not mean to imply that the natural sciences such as geology and biology require no more intellectual respect from us than the special creation legends of Cherokee and Christian. The Book of Genesis, while rich not only in poetry (at least in the Elizabethan translation), but also in psychological truths about the nature of humankind, as speculation about the origin of life and the natural world, is, like its companion fable from Cherokee myth, not merely implausible and unverifiable but, what is much worse, dull. That is, like all mere fantasy, it is not interesting. Even children pause only briefly over these stories, which were invented by adults primarily to appease and get rid of annoying interrogations from knee-high midgets.

What the sciences have to tell us, on the other hand, about the nature and origin of things begin in most cases with events and objects which each man can perceive and verify for himself. Earthquakes can be felt; volcanoes are available, from time to time, for personal inspection (I would like to be an inspector of volcanoes); the results of erosion can be seen with the naked eye on most

any red-clay Tennessee hill farm; and such improbable objects as dinosaur skeletons confront us with the inescapable reality of earth's antiquity and life's marvelous strangeness, which even in its simplest forms exceeds the power of unaided imagination to conceive.

When the scientist goes beyond the immediately observable, however, no matter how cautious his suppositions and methodical his procedure, to construct a rational version—or an inspired vision—of what is and what has happened, then he is stepping from the direct knowledge available to our senses to the indirect knowledge created by our powers of reasoning. As such, however plausible his hypothesis and highly probable its truth, it is not infallible. It is not certain. And the further he moves beyond our direct experience the less certain become his conclusions.

I am aware that some technicians of the understanding maintain that sensory knowledge too is indirect, since, as they say, it comes to the mind "through" the senses. But this is a distinction we need not accept. Mind and the senses are one and the same. The eye is part of the mind, as is every fingertip, every sensitive cell of the body. The disembodied mind belongs in the same category of being as the griffin, the centaur and the Cherokee buzzard which created the Appalachian Mountains by the flapping of its wings.

Let me conclude this overlong digression by saying that I accept the intellectual constructions

by which the geologists attempt to explain the origin and character of the Great Smokies. All that I am attempting to do is to cast upon these formulations the faintest shadow of a doubt. Only a shadow. The evidence for their probable truth is powerful. Nevertheless it is at best a probable truth; the theory of mountain building is, in the end, as I called it to begin with, a "construct."

Which goes on as follows:

After the period of rock-making in the Pre-Cambrian ages, and after the Appalachian revolution in the Paleozoic era, which formed the original mountain range, there followed the stage known as mountain-carving. In this process, which continues in our own time, the mountains are being gradually worn down by the patient forces of weathering and erosion. The present

---

The violet-blue flowers of the wild blue phlox (Phlox divaricata) *are shaded by the Mayapple or mandrake* (Podophyllum peltatum).

Neither the continental glaciers nor the flooding of ancient seas greatly disturbed the Southern Appalachians, and it is primarily for these reasons that the Great Smokies are in the heart of what botanists call the vegetation cradle of North America.

landscape of the Smokies and of the Appalachian range in general is explained as the cumulative result of ages of sedimentation, followed by a briefer period of crustal folding and upheaval, followed by the third and present stage of erosion and downcutting.

The great ice sheets of Pleistocene time reached only as far as the Ohio River, and there is, therefore, no evidence of glaciation in the Appalachians. The proximity of the ice, however, did have a climatic effect, making the mountains in all probability much colder and more barren than they are now. At present there is no timberline in these mountains; except for the heath balds, to be described later, they are forested to the summits. But 20,000 years ago, when the Ice Age ended and the great glaciers withdrew, the higher ridges may have been alpine in character, as the presence of boulders in the valleys suggests. It was at this time also that the spruce and fir forest, which is characteristic of Canadian latitudes, probably spread into the southern Appalachian highlands.

This concludes the geological history of the Big Smokies. What the future holds for the mountains, according to geology, is simply a long continuation of the present erosional downgrading which will end, presumably, given enough time and if the world lasts that long, with the Appalachians as we know them reduced to a more or less featureless peneplain—to no more, that is, than a gently rolling surface of rock and

field and forest (we hope) not much above sea level.

Always assuming, let us remember, that the geologists are right. Always assuming that they know what they are talking about.

For what, I ask again, do we really know? No more, I submit, than the man who wrote, two thousand? three thousand? years ago,

"One generation passeth away, and another generation cometh; but the earth abideth forever . . ."

All the rest is mystery.

Rhododendron maximum *grows in the deep shade of hemlock forests and in dense thickets bordering mossy brooks.*

The numerous species of trilliums are named from the Latin word for "three," for all their parts are in threes—three leaves, plus a single flower with three green sepals and three petals. But these spring flowers of moist woodlands vary in color and form, from deep red or purple to yellow to green to white. This is Trillium luteum, *the yellow-flowered toadshade with its mottled leaves.*

when faces called flowers float out of the ground
and breathing is wishing and wishing is having—
but keeping is downward and doubting and never
—it's april(yes,april;my darling)it's spring!
yes the pretty birds frolic as spry as can fly
yes the little fish gambol as glad as can be
(yes the mountains are dancing together)

when every leaf opens without any sound
and wishing is having and having is giving—
but keeping is doting and nothing and nonsense
—alive;we're alive,dear:it's(kiss me now)spring!
now the pretty birds hover so she and so he
now the little fish quiver so you and so i
(now the mountains are dancing,the mountains)

when more than was lost has been found has been found
and having is giving and giving is living—
but keeping is darkness and winter and cringing
—it's spring(all our night becomes day)o,it's spring!
all the pretty birds dive to the heart of the sky
all the little fish climb through the mind of the sea
(all the mountains are dancing;are dancing)

—e. e. cummings
("when faces called flowers
float out of this ground")

3. Appalachian Explorations

The Conquest of Clingman's Dome

In the morning, in the carefree mountain air, we arise, the girls and I, and take our breakfast. For myself eggs, country-cured ham, biscuits, more red-eye gravy and of course grits. Harmony grits. Suzie and Judy ballast their bellies with massive mountain flapjacks, God help us.

Off to the park. To Great Smoky Mountains National Park, one mile south. There is no entrance station, no fee to pay. Under the provisions of its establishment, this park at least shall never charge admission fees. Thank God.

Once inside the park boundary all billboards fall away, the trees appear. Even the beer cans have vanished from the shoulders of the road, and the rippling brooks are free of old shoes, discarded cars and ladies' underwear. The clear and icy water looks good enough to drink. It *is* good enough to drink, just as it is, an astonishing and wonderful thing in our America. And so the first thing I do is stop the car, go down to the stream and have a double handful. To drink water fresh and direct from its flowing source, especially here in the Eastern states, is a rare, sweet, ineffable experience. It takes you back, back, back, back to

---

The flowering of the showy orchis (Orchis specta-bilis) usually in late April—signals the time when spring wild flowers are at their peak in the Southern Appalachians.

the time of the mountaineers, to Audubon and Bartram, to the Indians.

We stop at the Sugarlands Visitor Center for a map and information, and to see, especially, the first traffic light ever installed in a national park. There it is, sure enough, at the junction with the road to Cade's Cove, red, yellow, green, stop, hesitate, go, the real thing, another wonder to behold. Now in December there is no need for this gadget, but one can easily imagine the great steel crustacean traffic jams of spring, summer and fall when the encapsulated multitudes come, in their lemming-like masses, to follow one another's tail pipes along the asphalt trails.

The solution? Simple enough. Keep cars out of the parks. Cars and all other forms of motorized locomotion. As I have suggested in another book,[1] *the national parks should be for people, not for machines.* Let the machines find their own national parks and keep out of ours.

Without any sense of self-contradiction, I drive my own little car up into the mountains. The road is here, I might as well make use of it, I've been taxed cruelly to help pay for it, I'd be a fool to walk and let the other motorists blow their foul internal-combustion gases in my face. But let me say I'd be only too happy to get out of this tin bug and walk, all the way to Newfound Gap, if all others were compelled to do likewise. I can imagine no greater sense of liberation than to drive my last automobile into the junkyard,

[1] *Desert Solitaire* (New York: McGraw-Hill, 1968).

there to watch it crushed to the size and shape of a footlocker, and never for the rest of my life see one of the miserable things again. *Freedom!*

Let us proceed. Upward. On all sides stands the quiet forest, lightly dusted with snow. All trees are leafless but the various oaks and the never-say-die American beech, *Fagus grandifolia.* The laurels and rhododendrons also keep their leaves through the winter but let them hang limp and loose, like the tongues of played-out hound dogs, in mute concession to the freezing cold.

Rushing torrents roar in the gulch, plunging beneath thick solid lids of ice on the rock-rimmed pools. Giant stalactites of ice, stained yellow by iron sulfides, hang from the stony cutbanks on the inside of the road. Clouds cover the highest peaks today, but the craggy flues of the Chimney Tops are clearly visible ahead and above. Waterfalls gush from caverns of ice. Snow on the boulders, green moss on old gray rocks.

I notice the oaks again. The peculiar conforma-

"You fling yourself on the ground, you drink, but you are too lazy to stir. You are in the shade, you drink in the damp fragrance, you take your ease, while the bushes face you, glowing, and, as it were, turning yellow in the sun."

—*Ivan Turgenev* (A Sportsman's Sketches)

tion of their branches. They have a startled look about them, as if electrified.

And everywhere throngs the laurel, the rhododendron, in dense stands taller than a man. The laurel hells, I've heard them called. Or laurel "hails," as they say down here. Where savage hunters lay for bear, as my friend Thomas Wolfe would say, and arrows rattle on the red oak leaves.

Higher and higher we rise, toward the clouds, the cloud forest. We reach a certain elevation, about 4,500 feet, where all of the trees are covered with a delicate, brilliant, impeccable snowy lace. Not snow, not ice, but frozen fog, that's what it is, as we discover on close examination. Brittle and fragile crystals of frost. Apparently the pine needles act as condensation nuclei, around which the cloud vapors gather and freeze. The effect is stranger than that of snow or ice; each tree, seen against the sun, seems to glow, to radiate an aura of intense white light. Halt—

Official roadside viewpoint. We stop and read the official roadside viewpoint warning sign:

WARNING
DO NOT FEED THE BEARS
Bears are dangerous when fed,
molested or approached closely.
Violators may be arrested.

To which some park visitor has added, "Or eaten."

Onward. We come to Newfound Gap, where the transmontane highway reaches its highest point before descending the other side of the mountain to the south and east, into North Carolina. Elevation 5,048 feet. Here the Appalachian Trail intersects U.S. 441. A sign on the trail says, "Mt. Katahdin, 1,823 miles."

Other cars are here, not very many. A carload of kids from Texas are throwing snowballs. Judging from their joy, they haven't seen snow on the ground for a long time. A stiff wind is blowing in from the north and the thermometer on the ranger's shelter reads 30° F. No day for a walk to Charlie's Bunion.

We drive the snow-covered road to Collins' Gap, end of the road, where the half-mile trail to Clingman's Dome begins. Through a winter wonderland. The wind has blown away the clouds and the sun stares down from a clear blue sky. The snow is everywhere, a dazzling diamond-field. Sleighs and sleigh bells would be appropriate on a splendid day like this. More cars at the trailhead. Honeymoon couples are busy stuffing snow down each other's necks. Such handsome lads, such lovely girls, it seems too bad their laughter must sound like the cackle of grackles. And the bray of mules.

I trudge the snow-packed trail alone, up through the silent forest of balsam and spruce. By balsam I mean, here, the Fraser fir, *Abies fraseri*. Near Clingman's Dome it grows in almost pure stands and in association with the red spruce, *Picea rubens*, which is also abundant at this alti-

44

tude. To find a comparable forest one would have to journey north into Canada. The trees form such dense stands that the forest floor is deep in shade, with little plant life. I see a few juncoes flitting about, a few titmice and chickadees, nothing else. In the snow I find the tracks of rabbit, birds and mice, a lone skunk. Blue shadows lie across the snow. In the stillness I can hear the melting of the frost crystals on the trees and their fall from branch to branch. Now there is not a whisper of wind.

The trail ends on the summit of the mountain at the highest point in the Great Smokies, 6,643 feet above the sea. Because the forest grows so thickly here, the Park Service has constructed an observation tower of reinforced concrete to enable the visitor to get above the treetops and see the world beyond. A long spiraling ramp leads from the ground to the top of the tower, which is about forty feet high and resembles a table lamp by Noguchi. I won't call it ugly; some might even think it beautiful; and certainly you could have a great wheelchair ride coming down that ramp, if you had a wheelchair. Let us say merely, gently, that here on Clingman's Dome, in the midst of the oldest, loveliest, woodiest forest in the eastern United States, it seems a little odd that any kind of structure, let alone a simple observation tower, should have to be built of *cement,* as if meant for a World's Fair exhibit on Flushing Meadow.

In any case, with the weather right, one gets a fine panoramic view from here. Waves of hills roll out in all directions, covered with forest and lightly veiled in that prevailing blue mist of vapor and distance that gives these mountains their name, and to the southwest, shining in the light, I can see man-made Fontana Lake.

The wind comes back, knifing into my neck. The Noguchi table lamp, all curves, not a square corner in sight, gives no shelter at all from any movement of the air. I skate down the Futuramic ramp, which is slick with ice, and walk back the trail through the snowy glitter of the forest. The air is full of floating particles of frost and snow, sparkling in the clear sunlight.

A Walk in the Woods to Alum Cave

An inch of virgin snow all over the ground— I am the first to walk this trail today. I cross the West Prong of the Little Pigeon River on a wooden footbridge, pausing in the middle of the bridge to admire the view upstream. It looks like a scene invented by Eliot Porter: granite-like boulders lodged in the torrent and sheathed in ribbed, rippled layers of ice; spillways and plunge pools, the roil and rush and roar of the complicated waters; giant hemlocks leaning over the stream, fresh snow clinging to their bark; the stones and pebbles of the creek bed gleaming through the flawless clarity of the water; and over all, illuminating the scene and blending with its shadows, the soft gray light of the humid mountain air, filtered by cloud and by the ran-

dom reticulation of the commingled tree branches and pine needles overhead.

Across the bridge, where trolls dwell. But I hear no knocking or grumbling below; I guess like the bears they've gone into hibernation for the winter. I sign my name in the registration book at the trailhead. I'm not only the first today, I'm the first in a week to come this way. How glad I am now that we decided to come down here in the dead of winter. On the wooden box that shelters the registration book, somebody has inscribed swastikas. Nazi swastikas. There's another good reason for coming here in the dead of winter. Easier to avoid the grim and silent majority.

In the foreground the hobblebush
(Viburnum alnifolium).

"Sound has called unto sound and the forest is all one mighty harmony. Is it deep organ music that strikes upon my ear, while fainter strains drift lingering among the arches of the trees? Brief silence falls. The aery music wakens anew and all about me there is a soft plaining, murmurings within murmurings every leaf has its own tongue; every blade of grass gives back its individual note."

— *François Chateaubriand (Diary)*

On the trail, the first thing I see of unusual interest is a big yellow birch that appears to have lifted itself about three feet out of the ground and to be standing aloft on its roots. This, I learn, happened because the seedling birch first took root on top of the decaying stump of another tree. As the stump disintegrated, the birch extended its roots into the earth but remained propped on them above the level of the ground, as if on stilts.

Turn and turn about. Here's a laurel taking root in the crotch of a dead birch. Leaves drooping. All the laurels and rhododendrons stand about with hanging leaves. It is indeed very cold. And damp. I am wearing a heavy coat, a fur hat, and writing these notes with gloves on my hands.

Walking up the snowy trail under the snow-laden trees, I feel an immense goodwill, despite the swastikas, toward my fellowman. Perhaps because I'm all alone. Anthropy, not misanthropy, is what I feel today. I feel a special benevolence toward the national park system and the Federal agency that administers that system. As a part-time employee of the Park Service, I have always been impressed by the high esteem in which the general public seems to hold this branch of the government and by the friendliness that it—the public—exhibits toward Park Service rangers and naturalists. Impressed and a little puzzled. Most of us most of the time feel toward the uniformed functionaries of the state, especially police and quasi-police like rangers, no more

47

at best than a grudging tolerance, as of a necessary evil. Why should the Park Service enjoy a special privilege in this regard?

Now, today, it seems to me that I have hit upon the answer. With Great Smoky Mountains National Park inspiring such pleasure and satisfaction, it occurs to me that the national park system is one of the very few decent things which the U.S. Government—that remote and faceless institution—has ever provided for ordinary citizens. Maintaining the park system is almost the only *nice, friendly* thing which the Federal Government does for ordinary people. Nearly all of its other activities, carried on at our expense, are for the benefit of the rich and powerful, or for the sake of secret, furtive, imperial causes that can inspire in us feelings only of sickness, shame and dread.

But the national parks belong to everyone. To the people. To all of us. The government keeps saying so and maybe, in this one case at least, the government is telling the truth. Hard to believe, but possible. The parks are communal property— even "hippies," the new bottom caste in our social hierarchy, are allowed to visit and camp in the national parks. (Though not, of course,

Near Cades Cove Road in the Tennessee Smokies.

without a little extra surveillance and occasional harassment by the "authorities.") Not only do the parks belong to the people, also hippies, they belong as well to that which came before us—to the wild things, to the wilderness. Emiliano Zapata said it exactly:

"The land, like the sun, like the air we breathe, belongs to everyone—and to no one."

A dead tree has fallen across the creek, forming a natural bridge. In the soft fresh snow on this bridge, I see the footprints—like tiny handprints—of a raccoon going halfway across, turning, coming back. Apparently he lost his nerve midway over the icy current. Or maybe he only changed his mind.

A giant birch looms beside the trail, encrusted with cankers; one of the cankers resembles a tragic mask, scowling horribly. Dead trees here and there, many of them, and on each are stacks of saprophytic fungi, big clamlike shapes tough and rubbery. Elaborate filigree of ice and crystal at the water's edge. Rocks coated with lichens, moss, frozen slime. I see the tracks of a small animal which has dragged something—its own tail? —across the snow into the brush.

High on the mountainside now, above most of the birch and hemlock, I come to what the mountaineers called a "laurel slick" and what the botanists call a "heath bald." Hard to see why one term is any more useful than the other. It is a treeless area on an exposed shoulder of the mountain covered with a dense growth of shrubbery,

head high, most of it members of the heath family—mountain laurel, rhododendron, sand mrytle, blueberry. The complete absence of trees in such places as this in the otherwise well-forested Smokies has not been satisfactorily explained, but the park naturalists assume as probable cause a natural catastrophe, such as fire, windfall or landslide, which wiped out the trees a long time ago and allowed the heath family to take their place. Perhaps eventually the trees will work their way back and resume their climactic place in the natural order here.

Trails like tunnels burrow through the thicket.

Clingman's Dome.

"It is not so much our technical or mechanical terms that need extending but ourselves. We have a great deal of exploring to do in order to find the place where we share our lives with other lives, where we breathe and reproduce, employ our sight, and join the breadth of chances not as separate, unique entities with doomsday on our docket but as vessels for universal experience. What we call natural resources cannot be limited to gas, oil, pulpwood or uranium—we are starving the natural resources in ourselves. The soul still needs to stretch; being needs exercise."

—*John Hay ("In Defense of Nature")*

A man could hardly crawl through there on hands and knees. Far below me, in the foggy valley, crows are yawping. Good hiding place up here, I'm thinking. The thought recalls another old mountain song:

> *I'm gonna build me a cabin*
> *Up on the mountain so high*
> *That the blackbird can't find me,*
> *Nor hear my sad cry. . . .*

The sun is a pale white disc behind the flowing clouds. That big holy wafer in the sky. I'm a-gonna be fogbound pretty soon if I don't get myself down off this here smoky mountain. But first— Onward. Upward.

To Alum Cave, which is not a cave but a great overhanging bluff maybe a hundred feet high. The brow of this bluff is festooned today with curtains, chandeliers, draperies, fangs and tiers of gigantic icicles, massive sabers of ice ten to twenty feet long. If one of those were to drop on a man, it would cleave him from head to toe. I retreat beneath the shelter of the overhang and look out over the valleys, into the clouds, feeling as if I were inside the gaping mouth of Leviathan, peering outward past his teeth.

How strange and wonderful is our home, our earth, with its swirling vaporous atmosphere, its flowing and frozen liquids, its trembling plants, its creeping, crawling, climbing creatures, the croaking things with wings that hang on rocks and soar through fog, the furry grass, the scaly seas. To see our world as a space traveler might see it, for the first time, through Venusian eyes or Martian antennae, how utterly rich and wild it would seem, how far beyond the power of the craziest, spaced-out, acid-headed imagination, even a god's, even God's, to conjure up from nothing.

Yet some among us have the nerve, the insolence, the brass, the gall to whine about the limitations of our earthbound fate and yearn for some more perfect world beyond the sky. We are none of us good enough for the sweet earth we have, and yet we dream of heaven.

Bitter as alum. Lonely laughter in the mountains. Read the official description to the people, they're out there somewhere, I can hear them breathing:

"Ground waters seeping through the rock have picked up mineral matter and deposited it on the face of the bluff in the form of alum. Only a thin film, it is not of commercial importance. Nevertheless a persistent legend has it that saltpeter was found here in considerable quantities during the Civil War and converted into gunpowder."

We're close to a mile high, up among the balsam and the spruce again, evening and fog are creeping close. I watch the tip of a slowly dripping icicle near my nose. Slower and slower the water oozes down. When that last drop freezes on the point, it will form a little bulb, like the button on a fencing foil. Ice daggers, glassy

swords and crystal knives crash around me. Time to go.

Out yonder in the purling mist a lank and long-connected bird, dark as a shadow, comes drifting slowly toward me, scarcely moving his black wings. Time to go.

The Travels of William Bartram

Appalachia, like America, was discovered by the Indians. Might as well keep that in mind, in case those people give us trouble again. Next to explore the region but not to settle were the Spanish, who, under the command of De Soto, penetrated Cherokee territory in southern Appalachia in 1540, seeking as usual gold and silver and offering the Indians in return the pox and slavery. Unsuccessful in his quest, De Soto died of malaria on the banks of the Mississippi. He is remembered today by most Americans as a large, unreliable automobile that was phased out of production in 1959.

After the Spanish came a century or so of relative peace for the Indians, from our point of view merely a lacuna in the march of history, followed

---

Reminiscent of the shamrock, the common wood sorrel (Oxalis montana) *is a Canadian-zone plant that has adapted to the cool damp woodland floor of Southern spruce-fir forests.*

in the eighteenth century by us, the English, the pale-faced hordes pushing in from the coast in human waves, certain doom for the Cherokee and all other Indians east of the Mississippi.

An exception to the new predatory type was one William Bartram, a remarkable botanist, writer and traveler, who journeyed on horseback, mostly alone, through much of the Carolinas, Florida and Georgia in the years immediately preceding the American Revolution. One of the first of the great American plantsmen, a trained naturalist and a close observer of the world he lived in and traveled through, Bartram wrote a book about his experiences and discoveries that is considered a classic in the realm of travel literature. Published in Philadelphia in 1791, in London the following year, the book was read and much praised by such celebrities of the time as Carlyle, Coleridge and Wordsworth. Both poets are supposed to have written some of their most famous work under the influence of Bartram's descriptions of an idyllic, unspoiled, original America. It is easy, reading Bartram now, to see how strongly he must have appealed to the budding Romantic temper of that period. Whether describing Indians, alligators or carnivorous plants, Bartram portrays a native and natural scene where (almost) every prospect pleases and only (European) man is vile. And yet his accuracy and precision of detail, the unselfconscious sympathy for his subject, make the pictures of "lost, wild America" which he gives us very convinc-

ing. Here for example is his portrait of the Venus's flytrap, those "sportive vegetables," as he calls them:

Astonishing production! see the incarnate lobes expanding, how gay and sportive they appear! ready on the spring to intrap incautious deluded insects! what artifice! there behold one of the leaves just closed upon a struggling fly; another has gotten a worm; its hold is sure, its prey can never escape—carnivorous vegetable! Can we after viewing this object hesitate a moment to confess that vegetable beings are endued with some sensible faculties or attributes, familiar to those that dignify animal nature; they are organical, living and self-moving bodies, for we see here, in this plant, motion and volition.[2]

One thinks of current researches in the plant kingdom, where some investigators believe they have discovered evidence of sentient feeling, even emotions of pleasure and fear, in certain plants. Shelley was certainly not the first to speak of "the sensitive plant."

Bartram had eyes; the man really saw what he was looking at, as is shown in this description of a climbing vine:

What power or faculty is it that directs the cirri of the Cucurbita, Momordica, Vitis, and other climbers toward the twigs of trees, shrubs and other friendly support? we

[2] *Travels of William Bartram*, reprint edition (New York: Dover Publications, Inc., 1955), p. 19.

Flowering dogwood (Cornus florida).

see them invariably leaning, extending, and like the fingers of the human hand, reaching to catch hold of what is nearest, just as if they had eyes to see with; and when their hold is fixed, to coil the tendril in a spiral form, by which artifice it becomes more elastic and effectual, than if it had remained in a straight line, for every revolution of the coil adds a portion of strength; and thus collected, they are able to dilate and contract as occasion or necessity requires, and thus by yielding to, and humoring the motions of the limbs and twigs, or other support on which they depend, are not so liable to be torn off by sudden blasts of wind or other assaults . . .[3]

In his Appalachian travels Bartram discovered and named the flame azalea (*Rhododendron calendulaceum*), one of the most spectacular flowering shrubs of the Big Smokies and neighboring mountain areas:

The epithet fiery I annex to this most celebrated species of Azalea, as being expressive of the appearance of its flowers, which are in general of the color of the finest red lead, orange and bright gold, as well as yellow and cream color; these various splendid colors are not only in separate plants but frequently all the varieties and shades are seen in separate branches on the same plant; and the clusters of the blossoms cover the shrubs in such incredible profusion on the hillsides that suddenly opening to view from dark shades, we are alarmed with apprehension of the hill being set on fire. This is certainly the most gay and brilliant flowering shrub yet known . . .[4]

In trying to imagine what our country must have been like two hundred years ago, before the black plague of commerce, industrialism and urbanism laid its fatal curse upon the land, we could

Left to right: Strawberry (Fragaria), *Pineland Daisy* (Chaptalia tomentosa), *Violet* (Viola enarginata).

Detail of large drawing, Venus Flytrap (Dionaea muscipula), *lower left.*

[3] *Ibid.*, p. 19.
[4] *Ibid.*, p. 264.

Franklin's Tree (Franklinia Alatamaha).

Above: Custard Apple (Asimina obovata).
Below: Anona (Asimina pygmaea).

Sweet Shrub (Calycanthus floridus).

Trumpets (Sarracenia flava).

Left: Ogeechee Tupelo (Nyssa ogeche).
Right: Hawthorn (Crataegus).

Left: Pitcher Plant (Sarracenia minor).
Right: Butterwort (Pinguicula caerulea).

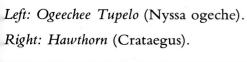

do worse than review what appeared to the candid eyes of such an honest and disinterested observer as William Bartram. The rivers and landscape of the southern Appalachians, now befouled and obscured by the wastes of pulp mills and dreary cities, scarred and torn by strip mines and freight-truck highways, looked like this in 1773:

I travelled some miles over a varied situation of ground, exhibiting views of grand forests, dark detached groves, vales and meadows, as heretofore, and producing the like vegetable and other works of nature; the meadows afford-

---

"For a great tree death comes as a gradual transformation. Its vitality ebbs slowly. Even when life has abandoned it entirely it remains a majestic thing. On some hilltop a dead tree may dominate the landscape for miles around. Alone among living things it retains its character and dignity after death. Plants wither; animals disintegrate. But a dead tree may be as arresting, as filled with personality, in death as it is in life. Even in its final moments, when the massive trunk lies prone and it has moldered into a ridge covered with mosses and fungi, it arrives at a fitting and noble end. It enriches and refreshes the earth. And, later, as part of other green and growing things, it rises again."

—Edwin Way Teale

(Dune Boy, The Early Years of a Naturalist)

ing exuberant pasturage for cattle, and the bases of the encircling hills, flowering plants and fruitful strawberry beds; observed frequently ruins of the habitations or villages of the ancients. Crossed a delightful river, the main branch of the Tugilo, when I began to ascend again, first over swelling turfy ridges, varied with groves of stately forest trees; then ascending more steep and grassy hillsides, rested on the top of mount Magnolia, which appeared to me to be the highest ridge of the Cherokee mountains, which separate the waters of the Savanna river from those of the Tanase [Tennessee] . . . This running rapidly a northwest course through the mountains . . . after being joined by a large river from the East . . . meanders many hundred miles through a vast country consisting of forests, meadows, groves, expansive savannas, fields and swelling hills, most fertile and delightful, flows into the beautiful Ohio, and in conjunction with its transparent waters [sic] becomes tributary to the sovereign Mississippi.[5]

For Bartram these were Elysian fields, and he so calls them, and their native inhabitants, the Cherokee Indians, who treated him always with courtesy, ceremony and generous hospitality, are described in his book as being very much what European Romantics had hoped and imagined, a race of natural noblemen.

"He was tall and perfectly formed," writes Bartram of one of many such princely Indian hosts; "his countenance cheerful and lofty, and at the same time truly characteristic of the red men, that is, the brow ferocious, and the eye active, piercing or fiery, as an eagle. He appeared to be about sixty years of age, yet upright and muscular, and his limbs active as youth."[6]

[5] *Ibid.*, p. 276.   [6] *Ibid.*, p. 285.

Alone and unarmed, Bartram moved freely among these warlike people, collecting his flowers and plants. In only one instance was he threatened by an Indian; in this case by a young warrior who had been mistreated and insulted by the white traders and was out to avenge himself at the expense of the first white he encountered. The first white was Bartram, who offered his hand in friendship, and the enraged Indian, after a few tense moments of hesitation, lowered his weapon and shook Bartram's hand.

Like John Wesley Powell a century later, Bartram not only trusted the Indians and earned their trust in return, he was seriously interested in their way of life, their customs, religion, society and economy. Treating them with respect, dignity and sympathy, he was able to learn far more about them than the traders and missionaries, who regarded the Indians primarily as raw material to be converted into profit or the traffic in souls.

In the eyes of the settlers who inevitably followed the traders and missionaries, the Indians had no value whatsoever but were merely another dangerous form of wildlife, like bear and lion, that had to be exterminated or removed in order to make the white man's occupation of the Indian's land secure. What William Bartram thought of the final stages of the tragedy of the Cherokee we do not know.

Rhododendron maximum. *The flowers of* Rhododendron maximum *vary from white to purple in color.*

Branches of Carolina hemlock (Tsuga caroliniana).

"Here in this wooded valley, mossy, cool,
   Where mountain water murmurs over stone,
   The jarfly sings upon a greenbriar stool
   A song I do believe is all his own.
   In this green mansion sunrays penetrate
   The trembling leaves between the earth and sky;
   The redbird sings a love song to his mate,
   And lazy winds mock singing bird and fly.
   To this green world I bring my Love with me
   And leave behind my gun and hunting hounds;
   And hand in hand we go as silently
   As snowbirds over winter's frosted ground.
   How can we sing a love song when we hear
   The barking squirrel, the redbird's love-song voice,
   The water, wind, the jarfly's lonesome churr?
   We listen to the love songs of our choice."

                           —*Jesse Stuart* (*"Valley Love Songs"*)

Before the arrival of the Colonials, Cherokees were the people of the Southern Appalachians. They farmed the bottomlands, repelled De Soto's raiding parties, hunted deerskin, and gathered the land's rich flora for European plantsmen.

"About 1790," Peter Farb writes, "the Cherokee decided to adopt the ways of their White Conquerors and to emulate their civilization, their morals, their learning, and their arts. The Cherokee made remarkable and rapid progress in their homeland in the mountains where Georgia, Tennessee, and North Carolina meet. They established churches, mills, schools, and well-cultivated farms; . . . In 1821, after twelve years of hard work, a Cherokee named Sequoya (honored in the scientific names for the redwood and the giant sequoia trees in California, three thousand miles from his homeland) perfected a method of syllabary notation in which English letters stood for Cherokee syllables; by 1828 the Cherokee were already publishing their own newspaper. At about the same time, they adopted a written constitution providing for an executive, a bicameral legislature, a supreme court, and a code of laws.

"Before the passage of the Removal Act of 1830, a group of Cherokee chiefs went to the Senate committee that was studying this legislation, to report on what they had already achieved in the short space of forty years. They expressed the hope that they would be permitted to enjoy in peace 'the blessings of civilization and Christianity on the soil of their rightful inheritance.' Instead, they were daily subjected to brutalities and atrocities by White neighbors, harassed by the state government of Georgia, cajoled and bribed by federal agents to agree to removal, and denied even the basic protection of the federal government. . . .

"Some Cherokee managed to escape into the gorges and thick forests of the Great Smoky Mountains, where they became the nucleus of those living there today, but most were finally rounded up or killed. They then were set off on a thousand-mile march—called to this day 'the trail of tears' by the Cherokee—that was one of the notable death marches in history."

—Peter Farb (Man's Rise to Civilization As Shown by the Indians of North America from Primeval Times to the Coming of the Industrial State)

4. Appalachian People

The Indians

After allowing De Soto and his men to pass through their territories and on into the oblivion which they so richly deserved, the Cherokee and other Indians of the southern Appalachians enjoyed a hundred years of being left alone, doing whatever Indians do when they are not fighting for survival. Their first contact with the English settlers of the Virginia colony was in 1654 at a point on the James River now occupied by the city of Richmond. There was a battle, which the Indians won, but they were not to win many more after that.

There followed a century of erratic and sporadic struggle, with the Cherokee and their Indian allies being gradually pushed back toward and into the mountains. In 1761 they suffered a disastrous setback when Colonel Grant, with an army of 2,600, which included a number of Chickasaw and Catawba Indians, pushed into what remained of Cherokee territory and destroyed fifteen of their major towns (yes, the Cherokee lived in towns), together with the granaries and cornfields surrounding the towns. When the Indians tried to resist, they were defeated, and the survivors became fugitives in the mountains, living upon roots, killing their horses for food and suffering not only from hunger but from smallpox, which, like alcohol, deceitful treaties and a divide-and-conquer policy, served then as later as one of the white man's most successful weapons.

For a while the Appalachian Mountains served as a frontier and barrier between the whites on the east and the Indians on the west. But the

whites, constantly and rapidly growing in numbers, were soon pouring through gaps in the range—Daniel Boone!—and settling down on what was still, officially, according to treaty (as long as the grass shall grow and the rivers flow, etc.) the property of the Indians. What is a treaty? As Hitler often pointed out, merely a scrap of paper. When one treaty was violated and the Indians rebelled, they were put down by force and mollified for a time by the drawing up of a new treaty, which was supposed to be good forever, and which reduced the Indian possessions still further. The process was carried on step by step, limited only by the limitations of the whites' military power, until, in 1828, with the election of Andrew Jackson to the Presidency, the fate of the Cherokee was sealed.

Old Hickory, frontiersman and Indian-hater (like most frontiersmen), by his mere election to the nation's highest office, gave the Indian exterminators and removers all the encouragement they needed. On December 20, 1828, one month after Jackson's election, the state of Georgia passed an act that annexed all Cherokee territory within her chartered limits; all laws and customs established among the Cherokee were declared

A low-growing rhododendron.

null and void, and no person of Indian blood or descent was to be allowed to act as witness in any suit where a white man was the defendant; all contracts between whites and Indians were ruled invalid unless established by the testimony of two white witnesses, which had the practical effect of canceling all debts owed by whites to Indians; the remaining Cherokee lands were mapped and divided into homesteads of 160 acres each and distributed by sale and lottery among white Georgians, except that each Cherokee head of a household was allowed to retain 160 acres (of his own land) but without any legal title; finally, the state made it a crime, subject to imprisonment, for any Indian to resist the seizure of his property, even his house, by a white. At the same time the Cherokees were forbidden by law to hold councils, to assemble for any public purpose or to dig for gold upon their lands. In short, the luckless Indians were deprived of both property and legal rights at the same time, and exposed to the mercy of the settlers' avarice. Still not satisfied, the states of Georgia and North Carolina began measures to secure the complete eviction of all Indians from their ancient homelands. These efforts, bitterly resisted by the Cherokees in every possible way, including appeals to the United States Supreme Court, achieved their aim in the years 1838–39 with what is called, in schoolbook histories, The Removal, and what is called by the descendants of the victims, The Trail of Tears.

What happened to these people is something

that will no doubt seem incredible to those who have been exposed to only the conventional and academic interpretations of American history. A certain General Winfield Scott was sent, with U.S. troops, into what remained of Cherokee territory in the Appalachian states, with orders to round up the Indians, assemble them at gathering points, like so many cattle, and from there march them westward into Oklahoma, a region which at that time was still far enough away to lie beyond the immediate appetite of the white Americans. The orders were carried out, firmly and ruthlessly. Men, women and children were surprised in their homes, surrounded with bayonets, herded into stockades. Those who resisted were destroyed on the spot; a few managed to escape and flee into mountain hideouts. One of those who succeeded in escaping was an old Indian named Charley, who together with his wife, his sons and a few friends broke out of the net, killing one soldier in the act, and fled to a mountain hideout. Unable to round up Charley and the other fugitives, General Scott offered to allow the others to remain in North Carolina if they would surrender Charley and his sons for punishment (for the killing of the one soldier). Upon hearing of this proposition, Charley and his sons gave themselves up voluntarily in order to secure amnesty for their companions.[1] Charley was ex-

[1] Another, possibly more authoritative account suggests that Charley, or Tsali—his Indian name—never gave up but was captured.—Ed.

ecuted, along with all of his sons but the youngest. The remainder of the fugitives, after many years of legal appeal, were finally allowed to remain in the Appalachian area; these were the ancestors of the present small tribe of eastern Cherokee, now settled on the Qualla Reservation around the town of Cherokee in North Carolina.

The main body of the Cherokees, however, some 17,000 men, women and children, were granted no mercy. The work of removal, as it was called, was carried out. A first group of Indians, about 5,000, were marched to various points on the Tennessee River, shipped by steamer down the river to the Ohio and the Mississippi,

---

Spinulose woodfern (Dryopteris austriaca).

"In autumn one is not confused by activity and green leaves. The underlying apparatus, the hooks, needles, stalks, wires, suction cups, thin pipes, and iridescent bladders are all exposed in a gigantic dissection. These are the essentials. Do not be deceived simply because the life has flown out of them. It will return, but in the meantime there is an unparalleled opportunity to examine in sharp and beautiful angularity the shape of life without its disturbing muddle of juices and leaves."

—Loren Eisely (The Immense Journey)

and from there marched again overland to their reservation in Oklahoma. The remainder, about 12,000, starting later in the fall of 1838, made the entire journey by land, a distance of more than a thousand miles, arriving in Oklahoma in March of 1839. It is estimated that nearly one-third of the second group, or approximately 4,000 persons, died on the march.

Eyewitness accounts of this exodus are available. Here are excerpts from the story of the affair as recalled by Private John G. Burnett, 2nd Regiment, 2nd Brigade, Mounted Infantry, U.S. Army. He called it his "Birthday Story," and addressed it to his sons and grandsons.

Children:

This is my birthday December the 11th 1890, I am eighty years old today . . .

The removal of the Cherokee Indians from their life long homes in the year of 1838 found me a young man in the prime of life and a Private soldier in the American Army . . . I saw the helpless Cherokees arrested and dragged from their homes, and driven at bayonet point into the stockades. And in the chill of a drizzling rain on an October morning I saw them loaded like cattle or sheep into 645 wagons and started toward the west.

One can never forget the sadness and solemnity of that morning. Chief John Ross led in prayer[2] and when the bugle sounded and the wagons started rolling many of the children rose to their feet and waved their hands goodby to their mountain homes, knowing they were leaving them forever. Many of these helpless people did not have

[2] Although irrelevant to the morality of the matter, it may be of interest to remind the reader that these Indians were not only Christian, but also literate, with a written language of their own, a tribal newspaper and a tribal constitution modeled on ours.

blankets and many of them had been driven from home barefooted.

On the morning of November the 17th we encountered a terrific sleet and snow storm with freezing temperatures and from that day until we reached the end of the fateful journey . . . the sufferings of the Cherokees were awful. The trail of the exiles was a trail of death. They had to sleep in the wagons and on the ground without fire. And I have known as many as twenty-two of them die in one night of pneumonia due to ill treatment, cold and exposure. . . .

At this time 1890 we are too near the removal of the Cherokee for our young people to fully understand the enormity of the crime that was committed against a help-

[OVERLEAF]
A view south into North Carolina from the Tennessee Smokies.

The ancient mountains of the Blue Ridge Province extend from Georgia to Pennsylvania and include The Great Smokies, which provide the highest elevations in the East. What we see today are tree-covered cores of once giant, three-mile-high mountains— today's cores are granite, schist, gneiss and marble, some of which are one billion years old. To the west of the Blue Ridge Province are the Ridge and Valley Provinces and the Cumberland Plateau. Unlike the Blue Ridge, these younger and smaller ranges have not lost their sedimentary cover and are rich in sand-

stone and shales, limestone and infolded beds of coal.

For the better part of 125 years following the American Revolution, the mountains isolated the Southern Highlanders. As Harry Caudill puts it: "The world ignored the mountaineer as he ignored it. Perhaps the first mention of the Southern highlander in American literature appears in a tale by Edgar Allan Poe in which he referred to the 'fierce and uncouth races of men' dwelling in Western Virginia.

"When Horace Kephart came to North Carolina from New England early in this century, he was astounded to find an entire segment of the American people about whom there was no literature. He could find not even so much as a magazine article written within the preceding generation to describe the Southern highlands and their inhabitants. He found no histories or novels that showed an intimate local knowledge of either. He declared, 'Had I been going to Teneriffe or Timbuctu, the libraries would have furnished information aplenty; but about this housetop of eastern America they were strangely silent; it was terra incognita.'

"Kephart remained in the Great Smokies for many years and in 1913 published Our Southern Highlanders, *almost certainly the best commentary to date on Poe's 'fierce and uncouth races of men.' His characters lived in the shadow of Clingman's dome, Mount Mitchell, Guyot, Le Conte and the Blacks, but they were of the same breed and stamp as the people farther west in the smaller mountains of Kentucky.*

"And in the half century that followed Kephart's work, the mountaineer was betrayed countless times. To begin with, he was betrayed by his ancestors who foolishly sold a gigantic wealth of timber and minerals for only a few pennies to the acre, thus effectively disinheriting whole generations. He was betrayed by the timber barons who exploited the forests with remorseless cupidity, and by the coal corporations which emptied and scarred his hillsides, contaminated his streams with mine acids, polluted his air with sulfurous fumes from burning culm heaps, maimed thousands of workmen and spread multitudes of widows and orphans across the valleys. He was betrayed by his politicians who conspired with the great, absentee-owned extractive industries to permit them to withdraw the riches of the mountains without being taxed to provide the schools, libraries, hospitals, and other services for which the mountaineers hungered. He was betrayed by the mission schools and colleges which came to educate his children and taught them to leave the region rather than to stand and fight for its development or, in the case of those few who actually remained, failed to inspire them to lead their people in the building of a society worthy of their heritage. And this betrayal is saddest of all, because in county after county the little cadre of lawyers, doctors and politicians who can boast of a college education are generally staunch defenders of the status quo and of those who plunder the region. Rarely is one encountered who advocates the cause of the mountaineer or his land."
    —Harry Caudill (Foreword to

    John Fetterman's Stinking Creek)

less race, truth is the facts are being concealed from the young people of today. . . .

. . . Murder is murder whether committed by the villain skulking in the dark or by uniformed men stepping to the strains of martial music. Murder is murder and somebody must answer, somebody must explain the streams of blood that flowed in the Indian country in the summer of 1838. Somebody must explain the 4,000 silent graves that mark the trail of the Cherokees to their exile. I wish I could forget it all, but the picture of 645 wagons lumbering over the frozen ground with their Cargo of suffering humanity still lingers in my memory.

Let the Historian of a future day tell the sad story with its sighs its tears and dying groans. Let the great Judge of all the earth weigh our actions and reward us according to our work.

Children—Thus ends my promised birthday story. This December the 11th 1890.

The Mountaineers

With all but a remnant of the Indians either dead or exiled from their Appalachian homeland, the way was clear for white settlement. Beginning in the 1790's, as the red men were gradually eliminated, descendants of the original English and Scotch-Irish colonists moved deeper and deeper into the mountains. The first arrivals naturally occupied the choicest farmland, the valley bottoms and "coves" between the high ridges; their descendants, as families grew in size, were then forced to move higher into the narrow valleys, up along creek branches and onto the steep hillsides. There was nowhere else to go, if they wished to remain, as most of these clannish

people did, in the neighborhood of their parents, grandparents, brothers, sisters and other relations. Pressing against the limits of subsistence, like the Indians before them or any other biological entity, the early mountaineers suffered an inevitable decline in their economic standard of living, but developed in response a culturally stable way of life adapted to the physical environment.

Meanwhile the mainstream of American life passed by these mountaineers, flowing around the rough and profitless Appalachian Mountains in pursuit of the much more easily exploitable wealth of the Midwest and the Far West. For over a century the mountaineer settlements were left in cultural and economic isolation, an island or backwater overlooked and forgotten by the managers of the great industrial development which was and still is altering the face of a continent.

Left to themselves, cut off by lack of easy transportation and communication from the majority of Americans, the mountaineers retained much of their old manners, speech and customs, and developed others peculiar to themselves. Lacking doctors, out of touch with anything resembling medical science, the mountain people learned to find remedies for their ills in the herbs and roots that grew in the forested hills around them. Without the cash to buy tools or manufactured goods, and too far anyhow from the towns and cities where such things were available, they learned to make do with what they had or do without, and under the pressure of this necessity perfected their own crafts and arts.

When a mountaineer, for example, came down with yellow jaundice, or "yaller janders," his pharmacological lore prescribed a mixture of "sow bugs," a species of insects found under rocks around the cabin, and molasses. Bloodroot and sassafras tea were good tonics for the blood. For "female troubles," borrowing from Indian tradition, the lady pioneers brewed teas of smooth sumac, or brown cedar, or milkweed, squaw-weed, black haw, yarrow, rock fern and the inner bark of pine. For the heart, a tea made from lily-of-the-valley roots was considered helpful; another remedy was the purple foxglove, a plant that contains digitalis. Pokeberry wine was thought good for rheumatism. Living in the southern Appalachians, with the greatest variety of plants to be found anywhere in North America, perhaps in the world, it was not difficult for the mountaineers, combining Old World and Elizabethan herbal lore with what they were able to learn from the Indians and from their own experience, to find or invent a natural remedy or a sickbed comfort (cocklebur tea for a sore throat) for most every kind of misery flesh is heir to.

Lacking manufactured articles, these mountain pioneers made their own. Tools where possible were made of wood, or hand-forged with scrap metal. Their cabins and farm buildings were made from local timber, the logs split or squared off by hand, and joined at the corners by notch and chamfer joints, locking the logs in place. Home-grown wool was carded, spun, woven into cloth. Mills for grinding sorghum cane, and corn and other grains, were put together by hand, using native materials. Such things as hinges, latches and even bear traps might be made of leather, or whittled out of wood, or hammered together with odds and ends of wood and metal. Iron, a precious commodity, was used over and over again in one form after another until it was completely worn out.

Each householder built his own home. First he erected a fireplace and chimney, constructed of massive stone from the homesite and chinked with clay. By splitting a log in half and taking slabs from each half, the mountaineers obtained "matched" logs, and these, notched and locked at the corners, formed the walls. With a maul and wedge, or "frow," pin oak logs were split, quartered and rived into shingles or shakes, and these covered the roof. The floors were made of puncheon slabs or planks hewn from yellow poplar, each of them three or four inches thick and three feet or more wide. Such cabins, when properly built, would last for a century.

Primarily farmers, the mountain people kept chickens and hogs, ran cattle on the grassy balds, did their plowing with oxen or mules, rode on horses and in wagons. Every family naturally kept a pack of dogs on the place, and venison, bear, rabbit, squirrel and wild turkey supplemented the usual vegetarian diet. Meat was

smoked or salted for storage, vegetables canned. Most families would also have at least a few apple trees, and the produce of these too could be stored for winter use or converted into cider, applejack and vinegar. The basic crop, however, was corn, which was easy to grow on the stony soil of the hillsides, did not require much cultivation, was convenient to store, being slow to spoil, and was adaptable to several uses: sweet corn made good roasting ears for family consumption; field corn helped feed the pigs, chickens and cattle. Mashed, fermented and distilled into whiskey, corn also served as the handiest of all cash

---

Rainbow Falls,
Great Smoky Mountains National Park.

"The earth insists on its intentions, however men may interpret them. Unity and use is what it asks. And use is what may be missing. To the degree that we become disassociated by our power to exploit from what it is we exploit, so our senses will become atrophied, our skills diminished, our earth-related vision hopelessly dimmed. Without a new equation in which natural and human need are together in eternal process and identity, we may be lost to one another, and starved of our inheritance."

—John Hay ("In Defense of Nature")

crops for the mountain farmer, whose way to market was long and arduous.

The economic utility of corn whiskey is easy to see. The raw material, whether shelled and sacked or still on the cob, makes a bulky load for long-distance transport by team and wagon down rocky creek beds, forest trails, muddy and rutted roads. Whiskey on the other hand is compact, a concentrated item for which there always was and always is a firm demand and a sound, reliable market. From the time of George Washington's Administration—remember the Whisky Rebellion—the people of the hills have utilized this simple method of converting their raw materials into a salable product.

> *Get you a copper kettle*
> *Get you a copper coil*
> *Get you some new-made corn mash*
> *And never more will you toil. . . .*

So goes the hillman's song, which even today retains some relevancy, but not so much as formerly. Two world wars and the Prohibition Era assured boom times for the moonshiner, who manufactures the booze, and the bootlegger, who distributes it, but with the passing of those periods came changing ways, the age of affluence, the invasion of the Appalachian hills by new highways and new communications. There are still some in the southern mountain region who prefer their tonic clear (or what Paracelsus called "the elixir of life") from good old two-quart

Mason jars, but they are a diminishing number. In addition to the general reasons already suggested, there has been a marked deterioration in the quality of moonshine since the Second World War. Part of this is attributed to haste in the manufacture and part to the use of inferior equipment, such as old rusty auto radiators instead of the traditional copper tubing, in the distillation process.

Economically self-sufficient, the mountaineers, by reason of their isolation from the urbanized America which was growing up beyond the hills, retained and maintained a culture of their own as well, in which their music, their peculiar brand of Christian fundamentalism, their manner of dress, even their modes of speech distinguished them sharply from the majority of Americans. Aside from newly landed immigrants in the ghettos of the big cities, the blacks of the rural South, and the surviving Indians in the Southwest, the Appalachian mountaineers formed what was probably the most close-knit and distinctive ethnic group in the United States. Inbred and interbred, they were close kin to one another not only through blood and speech and way of life, but also through their needs, their problems, their segregation from the rest of America—a segregation that was, certainly, to a great extent voluntary and deliberate. Horace Kephart, in his book *Our Southern Highlanders*, quotes the reaction of one mountaineer to his sojourn as a mill hand in the lowlands:

"I lied to my God when I left the mountains and kem to these devilish cotton mills. Ef only He'd turn me into a varmint I'd run back tonight. Boys, I dream I'm in torment; and when I wake up, I lay thar an' think o' the spring branch runnin' over the root o' that thar poplar; and I say, could I git me one drink o' that water I'd be content to lay me down and die."[3]

Nevertheless, despite their love of their mountain homes (no less intense, perhaps, than that of the Indians whom they had dispossessed), the separateness and independence of the mountain people were eventually broken down. Whatever the special virtues and advantages of their way of life, it cannot be denied that they suffered from poverty, disease and deprivation to an extent incompatible with the official and highly advertised

[3] Horace Kephart, *Our Southern Highlanders* (New York: Macmillan Co., 1922), p. 307.

"*The leaves faintly rustled over my head; from the sound of them alone one could tell what time of year it was. It was not the gay laughing tremor of the spring, nor the subdued whispering, the prolonged gossip of the summer, nor the chill and timid faltering of late autumn, but a scarcely audible, drowsy chatter.*"

—*Ivan Turgenev* (A Sportsman's Sketches)

American Way of Life. Thus they were susceptible to the allure of wage slavery in the cotton mills, to the welfare measures and public works projects of the New Deal in the 1930's, to the high wages offered by war plant work during the Second World War. Not merely susceptible but, like peasants everywhere in the world, *driven* to it, forced out of the hills and into the cities by their own familial fecundity, the surplus produce of which had nowhere to go except (literally and figuratively) down. It was possible to grow corn on a fifty-degree slope; but beyond that point a man took the risk of breaking his neck by falling out of his own cornfield, which was ridiculous. And the process begun by industrialism, developed by welfare and war, is now being firmly completed by the invasion of superhighways, by strip mining and by commercial tourism—that ultimate blow to human dignity.

The strip miners have not been the first large-scale despoilers of the Appalachian region. The lumbermen hold that honor, and their attitude is adequately summed up in the oft-quoted phrase "All we want is to get the most we can out of this country, as quick as we can, and then get out." The type is well-known; recent examples of their work can be seen in the California redwood forests.

Destructive though the loggers were, their depredations (now under some state and Federal control in the Appalachians) cannot justly be compared to that of the modern and contemporary strip miners. While the logger might leave in his wake a devastated wasteland of stumps and slashings, the land remained, with the power, through new growth, to regenerate itself and produce a renewed forest cover; but the strip miner, in disemboweling the earth itself on a large scale, overturning what he calls the "overburden," under which most of the topsoil is buried, sets back the process of regeneration for an indeterminate time—possibly for a century or

---

"May I be dead when all the woods are old
And shaped to patterns of the planners' minds,
When great unnatural rows of trees unfold
Their tender foliage to the April winds,
May I be dead when Sandy is not free,
And transferred to a channel not its own,
Water through years that sang for her and me
Over the precipice and soft sandstone . . .
Let wild rose be an epitaph for me
When redbirds go and helpless shikepokes must,
And red beans on the honey-locust tree
Are long-forgotten banners turned to dust . . .
I weep to think these hills where I awoke,
Saw God's great beauty, wonderful and strange,
Will be destroyed, stem and flower and oak,
And I would rather die than see the change."

—Jesse Stuart ("May I Be Dead")

longer. This is by no means the only result of his work.

Wherever large-scale strip mining is carried out, in western Pennsylvania, eastern Ohio, West Virginia, Kentucky, Tennessee, you will see these immense horizontal gashes carved across hillsides, with enormous slides of rock, clay, uprooted trees and other debris eroding away beneath each cut. In the midst of these battlefield locales (industry's war against nature) are pools and puddles of acid-poisoned water, destined inevitably to seep into wells, springs and streams in the vicinity, contaminating local water supplies.

The great spoil banks beneath each strip mine not only bury fields and forest, they sometimes even threaten the homes of those unfortunate enough to be living below. In some places these man-made avalanches of debris have actually crushed the houses on the lower slope; in others the poisoning of the water supply has been sufficient to drive out the inhabitants; in many others the people try to live and carry on in their tiny mountain cabins with the brow of a strip mine looming over them. Whatever happens, one thing is certain: the people who live or try to live in the area are the losers; most profits from these ravages go to outsiders, to the mine operators, to the heavy-equipment manufacturers, to the industrial beneficiaries of the cheap coal thus produced. Some local people are employed as truck drivers and equipment operators, but when a seam of coal has been completely excavated the

operation necessarily moves elsewhere, leaving behind a sterile wasteland of ruined hillsides, ruined streams, ruined homes, in which the out-of-work natives return to their now-customary life on the dole.

How could people be so helpless in the face of this devastating attack on their lives, homes and livelihoods? The story begins at the turn of the century, when mineral buyers representing bankers and businessmen in the northern industrial cities came to the Appalachian regions to buy, not land, but rights to whatever minerals lay beneath the land. These agents had no difficulty in persuading the gullible mountaineers, for modest sums in cash, to sign away their rights to the unknown wealth buried under their feet.

An essential part of the transaction was the

Maples alongside a mountain stream.

"We should be impressed by the beauty and fragility of the dynamic balance that has been preserved for so many hundreds of millions of years during which life has persisted on earth. And we should especially appreciate the shortness of our tenure on earth and use the powers we have so recently assumed to perpetuate, not destroy, the balance."

—*Eliot Porter*

agreement on the part of the landowner to what is known as a "broad-form deed." This interesting legal document not only gives the buyer of the mineral rights the privilege of extracting the coal from the farmer's land, it also gives him the option to remove that coal "by any means convenient or necessary," and through a final clause in the contract frees him, the buyer, from any liability whatsoever for damages that might be inflicted upon the farmer's land by the process of the mining operation.

Such mineral rights, on such vague terms, were sold for an average price of fifty cents an acre. In those days, seventy years ago, nobody had ever heard of or even imagined what we now call open-pit or strip mining. The mountaineers, thinking they were gulling the city slickers, thinking of nothing more damaging to their lands than the traditional mine shafts and tailing dumps, were happy to sell.

Strip mining in Appalachia began on a big scale in the early 1950's. A mountaineer might be notified one day that operations were about to begin, the next day bulldozers and power shovels would be ripping his land apart. If he protested, he would be shown the broad-form deed to which his father or more likely his grandfather had affixed an *X* in lieu of signature. If he took the issue to court, the court would do as courts generally do, rule in favor of the big operator against the little man by upholding the legality of the old contract. As Woody Guthrie said,

Some rob you with a six-gun,
Some with a fountain pen . . .[4]

Or as Shakespeare said in *Henry VI*, referring to the enclosure of the commons (appropriation of communal lands by the gentry of the time),

Is not this a lamentable thing, that of the skin of an innocent lamb should be made parchment? And that parchment, being scribbled o'er, should undo a man?

As many have found to their anguish, the legal force of a sheet of paper, or parchment, depends chiefly upon the identity of the principal beneficiary. If the beneficiary is a coal-mining combine, the paper is considered a legal instrument to be backed up by all the organized violence at the command of the state; if the beneficiary should happen to be, however, let us say a tribe of Indians such as the Cherokee or the Seneca, then even a treaty signed by President George Washington becomes no more than a scrap of paper.

All states but Kentucky have now outlawed the broad-form deed. But this reform comes too late. According to the Bureau of Mines, with figures now five years out of date, the following acreages have been "disturbed" (a departmental euphemism) by surface mining in the Appalachian states:

Kentucky, 119,200 acres; West Virginia, 192,-

---

[4] From "Philadelphia Lawyer" by Woody Guthrie, © 1949–61 by Michael H. Goldsen, Inc.

000 acres; Ohio, 212,800 acres; and Pennsylvania, 302,400.

That was as of January 1, 1965. Since then strip mining has continued at an increasing rate, due to the increasing demands for low-cost fuel, and is predicted to continue so for an indefinite time into the future unless some sort of brake is placed by law upon the abuse.

The mountain people have always been poor, by the standards of a prosperous commercial society. But up until recent times their way of life at least provided them with independence and the pride that goes with it, with the social security of kinship ties rigorously honored (no mountaineer would hesitate to shelter a fugitive from the law, for example, if that fugitive happened to be a blood relation), with the dignity and even beauty of a distinctive life-style offering striking relief from the grim homogeneity of contemporary urbanism. As evolutionists and ecologists have often testified and richly documented, the health of any organic community (or eco-system) requires for its stability both temporal variation and cotemporal diversity. The more we moderns attempt to mold all of nature and all living things, including ourselves, into a uniform technocratic (or technetronic) pattern the more we jeopardize our very survival. The Appalachian mountaineers, contemptuously called hillbillies by the ignorant, could have provided us with the model of one among many alternate ways of living. As is also true of the American Indians, there is much we could have learned—could still learn—from them. But the tendency of things—and things rule—is to wipe out nonconforming objects. In the technocratic system, people, like rocks and trees, are objects. Nothing more.

So, the mountaineers have had to go. After a hundred and fifty years of relative isolation, the community of the hill people has been broken down, first by the various arms of industrialism— the logging business, the cotton mills, the coal mines, the damming of the rivers—followed by the TVA, Alcoa and Oak Ridge (where even today a full-scale model of "Fat Boy," the atomic bomb that destroyed at least 70,000 human beings in Hiroshima, is kept proudly on public open-air shameless display for the edification of tourists and schoolchildren), with the long-run effect, contrary to advertising, of reducing the general standard of living of the native inhabitants. Neocolonialism. The intensified poverty resulting from industrial progress has brought in turn public welfare, reducing the people to a psychological dependency upon the agencies of a government over which they have practically no control. The final step in cultural breakdown is performed through commercial tourism, which diminishes the mountaineers like the Indians to the status of historical oddities, wax figures in labeled glass cases. In this part of the process the establishment of Great Smoky Mountains National Park has unfortunately played an am-

biguous, double role, for not only did the creation of the park necessitate the eviction of many highlanders from their homes (to be sure, not without monetary compensation), but it also inevitably attracted the forces of mass tourism, commercial tourism, industrial tourism, with the consequent degradation, mentioned above, of these people—Indians and mountaineers—to the rank of curiosities. This was not, of course, the intention of the founders of the park.

Red maples (Acer rubrum) *in new growth.*

*"And how fair is this same forest in late autumn. . . .
The damp earth is elastic under your feet; the high
dry blades of grass do not stir; long threads lie shining
on the blanched turf, white with dew. You breathe
tranquilly; but there is a strange tremor in the soul.
You walk along the forest's edge, look after your dog,
and meanwhile loved forms, loved faces dead and living, come to your mind; long, long slumbering impres-
sions unexpectedly awaken; the fancy darts off and
soars like a bird; and all moves so clearly and stands
out before your eyes. The heart at one time throbs and
beats, plunging passionately forward; at another it is
drowned beyond recall in memories. Your whole life,
as it were, unrolls lightly and rapidly before you: a
man at such times possesses all his past, all his feelings
and his powers—all his soul; and there is nothing
around to hinder him—no sun, no wind, no sound . . ."*

—Ivan Turgenev (A Sportsman's Sketches)

5. Appalachian Climax: The Great Smoky Mountains National Park

Shenandoah National Park and the Blue Ridge Parkway provide an introduction to Great Smoky Mountains National Park, which includes the heart and forms the climax of the Appalachian mountain world. Clingman's Dome is the second-highest point in the eastern United States, and for thirty-six miles the Great Smokies stand 5,000 feet or more above sea level. Both parks and the parkway preserve, in outdoor-museum fashion, relics and examples of the now fast-disappearing culture of the former mountain folk

Lichens, moss, and partridge berry.

who lived here. All three protect many features of prehistoric, geological and zoological interest (Great Smokies National Park, in particular, being famous for its generally genial bears). The Great Smokies are also laced with many attractive trout streams and a comprehensive network of fine hiking trails, including a segment of the Appalachian Trail; all three places provide campgrounds and picnic spots for the city-weary tourist; and for the incorrigibly motorized multitudes who apparently find satisfactory recreation in merely exercising their automobiles, the parks together with the parkway offer an elaborate system of comfortable, well-paved, automobile trails, suitable for even the most sensitive cars.

The central purpose in the establishment of Great Smoky Mountains National Park, however, was preservation of the greatest stands of virgin forest yet remaining in the eastern United States. Few regions in the North American Temperate Zone contain as diverse a flora as can be found here. According to Arthur Stupka, for twenty-five years chief park naturalist at the Great Smokies, the park includes "more than 1300 kinds of flowering plants, almost 350 mosses and liverworts, 230 lichens, and more than 2,000 fungi . . ."[1] In the plant kingdom the trees especially have brought fame to the Smokies and attracted botanists (as well as lumbermen) from all over the world, being remarkable not only for variety of species but for the great size of individuals. Among the about one hundred kinds of native trees in the park (the exact number being dependent upon whether or not certain shrubs of arboreal size, such as mountain laurel, are counted as trees), some twenty varieties, including red spruce, eastern hemlock, yellow poplar, Fraser magnolia and mountain silverbell belong in the category known as "champions," because of their record dimensions.

Groves of these great trees are found in most impressive proportions in the sheltered coves between the mountains, at elevations below 4,500 feet. Here are the beautiful hardwoods that once covered all of what is now the United States from the Atlantic shore to the Mississippi—the yellow

buckeye, basswood, white ash, sugar maple, yellow birch, American beech, black cherry, red oak and the cucumber tree or *Magnolia acuminata*. Here, too, before the blight struck, grew the American chestnut. (My friend Newt Smith, on his old farm near Tuckasegee, has a pigpen made of chestnut.) In the Greenbriar area of the park stands a cucumber tree greater than eighteen feet in circumference; not far away is a yellow buckeye sixteen feet around, a sugar maple over thirteen feet, a yellow poplar over twenty-four feet. All of these measurements were made at four and a half feet above the ground. They are no less impressive in height, many of them standing more than a hundred feet tall, some a hundred and fifty feet.

Above the cove hardwoods is the hemlock

[1] Arthur Stupka, *Notes on the Birds of Great Smoky Mountains National Park* (Knoxville: University of Tennessee Press, 1963), p. 11.

"Face it—you must—and do not turn away
From this bright day,
Intolerably glorious and bright,
Red-gold and blue by day, white-gold and blue by night.

Face it, and doing so,
Be wise enough to know
It is Death you face, it is Death whose colors burn
Gold, Bronze, vermilion in the season's turn."
—*Rolfe Humphries ("Autumnal")*

forest, another outstanding feature of the Great Smokies, and the northern hardwoods—yellow birch, American beech—which intergrade with the spruce-fir forests of the summits. In these three different plant communities, we find a variety of trees (and shrubs) that include within their outer limits as great a variation in flora as one would find in traveling from Tennessee to northern Canada.

Not yet mentioned but also found in the Smokies are other hardwoods—white oak, black oak, pignut hickory, red hickory, mockernut hickory, even a few shagbark hickories (common in the Allegheny Mountains), red maple, sweet birch, black gum and black locust—and five species of pine: shortleaf, longleaf, table-mountain (endemic), eastern white and pitch.

These primeval forests are beautiful at any time of the year—I like them even in winter, when the leafless branches of the deciduous trees sketch bare, delicate traceries of line against the neutral gray of the sky, in the manner of ancient Chinese brush and ink drawings—but it is of course in autumn when they attract the most attention. What happens then in the chemistry of leaves to produce those shades of coloring from subtle to brilliant that are the splendor and the glory of the Appalachian Mountains?

Part of the explanation is functional. In order to survive the freezing temperatures of winter, when water (because frozen) becomes unavailable, the leaf-shedding trees must go into a

dormant state. By shedding their leaves they escape a fatal loss of moisture. Far from symbolic of death, the leaves of autumn, like a snake's discarded skin, are signs of survival and potential renewal.

The leaf coloring is a part of the shedding process. During spring and summer the green of chlorophyll dominates each leaf, performing the vital synthesizing of sunlight and earth that underlies all life on this planet; but in autumn, as the tree gradually shuts down its waterlines and the sap ceases to flow, the production of chlorophyll stops with it. As the green wastes away from each leaf, the other pigments, red, gold, orange, which had been present all the time but covered by the green, are now revealed, and in their infinitely variable combinations with remaining chlorophyll and other pigments, such as the brown of tannin (most noticeable in oaks), the drying leaves produce the spectacle of an Appalachian autumn. The leaves die but the tree survives.

The conifers are able to dodge this complicated process because their wax-coated needles, con-

---

Sugar maple (Acer saccarum) *branch near Ramsey Cascade in the Tennessee Smokies.*

taining few stomata (pores), allow them to get through winter without excessive moisture loss.

Great Smoky Mountains National Park was not born without labor. As might be expected, the lumbering interests set up a fierce opposition, together with a few lodge and hotel operators already ensconced within the present boundaries of the park. The acquisition of timber holdings eventually required condemnation proceedings in a struggle that began in 1923 and was finally successful in 1940, when President Franklin D. Roosevelt formerly dedicated the park to "preserving and protecting the wild beauty and natural features of the area for all time."

No natural area is made safe from human avarice simply by making it a national park. While national park status serves to protect the Great Smokies from further mining and logging, it attracts at the same time the more insidious dangers of what I call commercial, or industrial, tourism, the chief characteristic of which is the mania for laying out roads. The Smokies have not escaped this form of exploitation. At present the park is traversed by three roads—one along the east boundary, one through the center at Newfound Gap, one through the west portion from Cade's Cove to Tapoco—and intersected, looped and penetrated at a number of points by various other roads, both paved and unpaved.

Not satisfied with this, the local tourist industry is pressing hard for another transmontane road across the west-central part of the park, from Tremont to Fontana Lake and Bryson City. Some officials of the Park Service are also understood to be in favor of this proposed road. As proponents of the project argue, true to form, "Why let all that beauty go to waste?" The only firm opposition to the new road has come, as might also be expected, from local and national conservation organizations, particularly The Wilderness Society. At the time of this writing (January, 1970), the issue is tied up in the courts.

The problem facing Great Smoky, like the other popular national parks, is overuse. In view of the tremendous demand, the park is obviously too small. There are two solutions: (1) expand the park by acquiring more land, probably by now an impossibly expensive and complicated procedure; or (2) expand the park by banning cars and all other forms of motorized travel within it.

Speed shrinks distance. Roads shrivel parks. Keep out the cars and you will make what is now a two-hour routine drive from Gatlinburg to Cherokee into something more like a two- or three-day expedition on foot, bicycle or horseback. Set a man on foot at the entrance to the park, at any entrance, with no means to proceed except by his own energy and inclination, and he faces a vista as wild and immense as that which confronted Hernando de Soto, William Bartram or Daniel Boone. What was an excursion becomes an adventure.

96

Americans need adventure, wholesome outdoor adventure I mean, not sick and corrupt forms like cowardly wars against little peasant countries, or billion-dollar blast-offs to the moon for the technetronic elite. Especially young Americans need an outlet for adventure. And the unique beauty of this proposal, from the point of view of fiscal-responsibility types like myself, is that it will not cost us taxpayers a cent, will in fact save millions of dollars now wasted on road upkeep and police work in what should be a wilderness area.

Now let us hear no nonsense about restricting the park for the use of a privileged few. Motorless tourism confers no privileges on anybody. Banning cars will not prevent a single tourist from penetrating the Great Smokies, whether on foot, on bicycle or on horseback, whether alone, with friends or in a guided tour, to the limit of his will and ability. What could be more democratic than that? What could be more quintessentially *American*? Or as my old man used to say, One man's as good as another if not a damn sight better.

True, some tourists will get lost, perhaps for good. But searching for them will give the park rangers something dignified and useful to do; they'll like that. Nor will the tourist industry now concentrated in towns like Gatlinburg on the edge of the park bear any loss; after the first enormous howl of outrage dies away, the businessmen there will be delighted to discover that the crowds will continue to come anyway, that the parking-lot business and horse-rental business will more than compensate for loss in gasoline sales, and that nonmotorized tourism will result in visitors staying much longer, eating much more country-cured ham, drinking much more ice-cold cider, in the long run spending just as much money or maybe even more money than they ever did before.

The elegant simplicity and dazzling utility of the ban-all-motors solution to park problems may blind some to its feasibility. It is feasible. It can be done. Eventually it will have to be done. All that is lacking at present is the will on the part of National Park Service officialdom. Or to phrase it more poetically, the guts. All it takes is a little guts. And this, or these, it is the duty of the park-supporting public to supply.

The berries of flowering dogwood (Cornus florida).

"In the midst of death and retreat, there were denials of the new season. The dark purple berries of the poke-weeds sustained many forest birds for the drastic new season to come. The dogwoods, with their profuse red fruit, would feed thousands of birds, and many migrants ate blackberries, which grew in stunted clumps on the peninsula. Foxes, chipmunks, and squirrels ate red chokecherries, red bunchberries, and viburnums; and with others, they also ate acorns, beechnuts, hickory nuts, winterberries, bittersweet, and smooth sumac fruit."

—*Frank Russell* (Watchers at the Pond)

American mountain-ash (Pyrus americana) *in fruit.*

"*I have an understanding with the hills*
At evening when the slanted radiance fills
Their hollows, and the great winds let them be,
And they are quiet and look down at me.
Oh, then I see the patience in their eyes
Out of the centuries that made them wise.
They lend me hoarded memory and I learn
Their thoughts of granite and their whims of fern,
And why a dream of forests must endure
Though every tree be slain: and how the pure,
Invisible beauty has a word so brief
A flower can say it or a shaken leaf,
But few may ever snare it in a song,
Though for the quest a life is not too long
When the blue hills grow tender, when they pull
The twilight close with gesture beautiful,
And shadows are their garments, and the air
Deepens, and the wild verry is at prayer,—
Their arms are strong around me; and I know
That somehow I shall follow when you go
To the still land beyond the evening star,
Where everlasting hills and valleys are:
And silence may not hurt us any more,
And terror shall be past, and grief, and war."
　　　—Grace Hazard Conkling ("After Sunset")

6. Appalachia, Good-bye

Time to check out of the Bearskin Motel. Churlishly I refuse to pay the extra charge for use of firewood, implying that I think it immoral and unethical for a hotel, even a motel, to advertise as this one does—"YUP, REAL FIRE-PLACES"—and then penalize the unwary lodger for not bringing his own firewood. The clerk, an insouciant Southerner, smiles and graciously accepts my refusal. The Great Refusal.

Judy salvages our laundry from the Snow White & The Seven Dwarfs Washateria (free Baptist literature on the walls) and we are off, once more up the mountain to Newfound Gap and down the other side into North Carolina and the town of Cherokee, Cherokee Capital of the World.

More charming and picturesque philistinism: The Wigwam Motel, with wigwams made of steel and concrete (try dragging *that* down the Platte, Mrs. Crazy Horse); a green stegosaurus made of chicken wire and plaster, leering at the passing motorist from the doorway of a curio shop where authentic Indian spears, made in Hong Kong, are offered for sale; The Mystery House, Closed for the Season; Frontierland—20 Rides & Shows, One Price; Deadwood Gulch; Fort Cherokee; Redskin Motel—50 Ultra-Modern Units; Honest Injun Trading Post (behind a

Snow-weighted Southern balsam fir (Abies fraseri).

gateway of totem poles); and the Twin Tepee Craft Shop. Exhilarating.

Accelerating, we come next to Sylva where I had lived the year before while teaching at the nearby University of Western Carolina.

Sylva must have once been a lovely town. Small, with a population of perhaps 5,000, nestled in the green hills below the Great Smokies, full of beautiful old houses, laved as they say by the sparkling waters of the Tuckasegee River, with the life of a market center and the dignity of county seat, Sylva must have been beautiful. Now it is something else, for the streets are grimy and noisy, jammed always with motor traffic, the river is a sewer, and the sky a pall of poisonous filth. The obvious villain in the picture is the local Mead's Paper Mill, busily pumping its garbage into the air and into the river, but general traffic and growth must bear the rest of the blame.

When I commented to one of the town's leading citizens, a fine old Southern gentleman, about the perpetual stink in the air, he replied, "Why, son, that there smells lahk *money* to me." Smug and smiling all the way to the bank, where—I hope—he drops dead on the doorstep. Pascal said somewhere in words to this effect that in order to grasp the concept of the infinite we need only meditate for a while upon human stupidity.

Looking at the foul mess industry has made of a town like Sylva, I am also moved to reflect, once again, that capitalism, while it sounds good in theory, just doesn't work. Look about you and see what it has done to our country. *Mene, mene, tekel . . .*

I don't know. One suffers from hope. Maybe we can learn something from what we have done to this land. Probably not. And in any case, is it any better elsewhere? No matter in what nation I lived I am certain I would find much to detest. All big social organizations are ugly, brutal, inhuman—prone to criminal acts which no man or *community* of men, on their own, would even think of. But just the same I despise my own nation most. Because I know it best. Because it is mine. Because I still love it, suffering from hope.

"*When I hear people say they have not found the world and life so agreeable or interesting as to be in love with it, or that they look with equanimity to its end, I am apt to think they have never been properly alive or seen with clear vision the world they think so meanly of, or anything in it—not a blade of grass. Only I know that mine is an exceptional case, that the visible world is to me more beautiful and interesting than to most persons, that the delight I experienced in my communings with Nature did not pass away, leaving nothing but a recollection of vanished happiness to intensify a present pain.*"

—*W. H. Hudson* (Better to Be)

Enough of these gloomy thoughts. We must hasten on to Tuckasegee, Judy and Suzie and I, to visit old Newt Smith and his marvelous chestnut pigpen again. And after that—home.

And where might that be? Where is home? That old gray gaunt Gothic farmhouse along a red-dog road in the hills of northern Appalachia? No more; never again. Where then?

A Russian writer named Prishvin said that "Home is where you have found your happiness." I think I know where that may be, at least for myself. I'll reveal this much: it has something to do with those mountains, those forests, those wild, free, lost, full-of-wonder places that rise yet (may they always!) above the squalor of the towns.

Appalachia, we'll be back.

Acknowledgments

For the Cherokee creation legend and the John G. Burnet account of the Cherokee Removal, I have borrowed from *Cherokee Legends and The Trail of Tears*, a booklet of adaptations of the original legends by Thomas Bryan Underwood, published by the S. B. Newman Printing Co., Knoxville, Tennessee.

My interpretation of the geology of the Great Smokies is based upon an article by Philip B. King and Arthur Stupka, "The Great Smoky Mountains—Their Geology and Natural History," published in *Science Monthly*, v. 71, pp. 31–43.

The quotations from William Bartram are from the Dover edition of his book, published in 1955.

For much of my information about the mountaineers I have relied upon Horace Kephart, *Our Southern Highlanders*, Macmillan Co., New York, 1922, and Michael Frome, *Strangers in High Places*, New York, Doubleday, 1966.

The song "*Copper Kettle*," partly quoted herein, is by Albert Frank Beddoe and was first published in his collection *Bexar Ballads from Bexar County, Texas*.

Information about the strip-mining problem is from David G. McCullough's "The Lonely War of a Good Angry Man," *American Heritage*, December, 1969, and that man is Harry M. Caudill, author of *Night Comes to the Cumberlands*, whose epilogue concludes this book.

Most of my information about the trees of the Great Smokies was borrowed freely from *Trees, Shrubs, and Woody Vines of Great Smoky Mountains National Park* by Arthur Stupka, Knoxville, The University of Tennessee Press, 1964.

For my summary account of Cherokee Indian history I am indebted to James Mooney, *19th Annual Report, 1897–98* (Washington, D.C.: Bureau of Ethnology, 1900).

For many of the materials used in the preparation of this essay, some of them otherwise unobtainable, I wish to thank the publisher of this book, John Macrae III.

For their patience in answering our many questions, my thanks to the naturalist staff, and particularly Glenn Cardwell, at the Sugarlands Visitor Center, Great Smoky Mountains National Park.

Finally and most of all my thanks to Judy and Suzie for coming along and helping out—they made it three times the fun.

Epilogue

Epilogue

By Harry M. Caudill

To know the ancient mountain range that parallels our Atlantic Coast is to love it. The Appalachians are a labyrinth of hills, mountains, broad valleys, narrow hollows, swift creeks, and splendid rivers. Its wrinkled maze is indescribably old—predating the Rockies by scores of millions of years. If one could enter a time machine and roll back the ages for 70,000,000 years, one would find growing in central Appalachia a forest remarkably like that of today. Here a generous but unhurrying nature perfected earth's finest expression of what botanists call "mixed-mesophytic forest." This vast mountainous domain is larger than Great Britain and, in its central core, botanists have counted more than 1,900 seed-bearing plants. Of these about 130 are classified as trees.

In the vast expanse of its history, this forest has inhabited a pleasant tangle of moist, warm hills and coves—a benevolent climate never too hot or too cold, too wet or too dry. So the immense woodland stabilized and the land adopted practically every plant and creature time and climatic change brought to it.

And a great number were brought—forced south by the glaciers which, in two great cycles, crunched down from the north along the mountains' outer rim, grinding into oblivion every living thing for thousands of miles. After the ice melted, seeds from the Appalachian storehouse spread northward again, following the dying glaciers as they dwindled toward the polar ice cap. They reseeded Canada and Alaska, then, by a now vanished land bridge, crossed into Asia and into the hills of eastern China. They left their

tracks in the rocks, and fossils tell us that today's forest in eastern China is an ancient descendant of our own Appalachians.

Its geological history filled the labyrinth with an incredible assortment of wealth to match its variety and beauty. Sometimes poplars acquired a diameter of ten feet. For thirty years the little hamlet of Louisa, Kentucky, was the world's largest market for hardwoods.

The decaying trees and the residues of immense canebrakes left ribbons of deep black soil along the creeks and rivers. The crystalline streams were continually renewed by the heaviest rainfall in North America, excepting only the rain forests of the Pacific Northwest.

But these merely cloaked an even vaster wealth —the minerals. *The Mineral Resources of Appalachia*, a detailed study issued by the Department of the Interior in 1968, discloses a breathtaking treasure, including coal, oil, gas, limestone, marble, granite, iron ore, copper silica, gneiss, mica, gypsum, talc, grahamite and gibbsite. The

---

". . . to breathe the keen frosty air, while half-closing the eyes involuntarily at the fine blinding sparkle of the soft snow; to admire the emerald sky above the reddish forest!"

—*Ivan Turgenev* (A Sportsman's Sketches)

deposits sprawl across the ancient range from end to end, and industrial man is determined to have them out and to convert them into automobiles, cosmetics, electricity, gasoline, warmth, paint, medicines, bottles, and tombstones, ad infinitum.

The settlers who drove the Indians out of Appalachia nursed a supreme distrust of government. They never developed a decent school system, and have steadfastly insisted on delivering public affairs into the hands of the most venal and uninspired politicians imaginable. Government remains weak and corrupt. The ancestors of today's mountaineers practically donated the title to most of the mineral deposits to speculators in the last quarter of the nineteenth century. Today those titles are held by corporations headquartered in New York and Philadelphia. The West Virginia Tax Commission warned in 1884 that the continued selling of such mineral and mining rights would transfer real sovereignty to the boardrooms of distant corporations, depriving West Virginians of control over their own destinies. If persisted in, said the commission, "The history of West Virginia will be as sad as that of Ireland or Poland." This grim prophecy has been realized in full measure. Extractive industries have hauled away monstrous quantities of ores, fuels, stones and wood—perhaps $500,000,000,000 worth in the last 130 years. According to the Interior Department the single most valuable mineral deposit in the world is the thick, heat-rich seam of coal stretching across western Pennsylvania, southwestern Virginia, West Virginia, and parts of eastern Kentucky. That seam has been mined by every method engineers and technologists have been able to devise.

Albert Schweitzer once gloomily declared that "Man has lost the capacity to foresee and to forestall. He will end up destroying the earth." It is ironic that as this book goes to press there is a worldwide wave of apprehension about the health of the world. Suddenly millions of people recognize with frightening clarity that the only life-supporting planet known to astronomy is under a sustained assault that threatens to destroy its intricate, interdependent eco-system. And as this recognition widens and spawns protest and calls for reform, it becomes increasingly doubtful that man can forestall the onrushing ruin. There is reason to believe that in his headlong rush from the caves to the moon he has locked himself within institutions that impel the suicidal repetition of the very acts which he now perceives to be deadly.

Under the law of medieval England, the land embraced not only the soil, the air and the water, but every living plant and creature upon or within them. This included people, so that even the harsh feudal system made strong exactions on the rulers to protect and perpetuate the otherwise rightless villeins. There was a wisdom in this that America has lost to her sorrow.

Modern America is presently committed to the endless proliferation of goods, growth based on ever-rising numbers of people, and a steadily mounting gross national product. In order to sustain its impetus, the American system makes incredible exactions upon the land. The requirements of unending expansion are rapidly depleting the entire continent of its metals and fuels.

Of course the results had to become apparent. The nation's stores of silver bullion will be exhausted at the present rate by the end of 1970. Copper prices have doubled in a year and a half

---

"Today our little world is clothed in snow
  Except for channels where the streamlets run;
  It stirs my brain to see the brilliant glow
  Of pouring high-hill streams beneath the sun
  That plow like ribbons of white-molten steel
  Down rugged valleys filled with blazing light.
  I shall go out and climb the highest hill
  Where I shall stay until approaching night
  To breathe deep down sun-softened atmosphere.
  My searching eyes will focus every scene
  From redbird on wind-sagging berry briar
  To snow still clinging to the winter-green
  Of swaying pines on ridges near the sky.
  I must possess before it does depart
  This world of winter beauty born to die
  To store for summer keeping in my heart."
          —Jesse Stuart

          ("Summer Keeping in My Heart")

and the price of molybdenum increased tenfold in 1969. Since we spew out goods in mounting waves without consuming our wastes, a once lovely continent has become clogged with junk, trash, and garbage.

In the ceaseless quest for goods and status, men have become so frantic to keep up with their fellows, and have so cluttered their communities with the effluvia of their civilization, that they must, to preserve some link with nature and some measure of sanity, repair at frequent intervals to yet unspoiled and uncrowded scenes. Thus the very social and economic system that sucks at the earth and rends it for its ores, fuels, crops, and lumber flings multitudes of men, women, and children across this same land in search of peace and spiritual restoration. Here are the twin forces that appear to doom the once magnificent Appalachians.

The prospect for Appalachia is sinister. It is already the nation's prime ecological disaster area. The hillsides will be rent by strip mines leveling forests, cutting deep and high gashes into the winding contours of ridge and mountain. Following the example set by contractors working for TVA in Breathitt County, Kentucky, entire ranges will be leveled layer by layer to "recover" fuel for steam plants and steel furnaces. The fragments of the dismembered mountains will be rolled into the valleys and the corpse of a forest with a once complex web of life will lie buried beneath a wasteland like the world as

described in the opening verses of Genesis—an Appalachian Sahara, an American Carthage plowed and salted.

Prodigious quarries will scalp other mountains for the silica-bearing crags of sandstone that sometimes stretch for a hundred miles. Other quarries will gnaw enormous notches into cliffs of limestone. The iron lodes around Cumberland Gap will be blasted from the beetling cliffs. Men digging for gibbsite, grahamite, and scores of other little-known minerals will plow the earth into wastelands comparable to Flanders when peace broke out in 1918.

The hill people have a strange relationship to their land. They find the hills haunting and fascinating, but their past is without a viable land ethic or any really deep comprehension of the earth. They have prostituted the land they love. Their relationship to their hills has been much like that of a man who sells his wife into prostitution: adoring her while pocketing her tawdry earnings. For generations they have been a people in flight. The onslaught against the earth will leave it so mutilated, so grimly ugly, so contaminated, silted, and defiled that the exodus will quicken.

Industry has always treated the mountains with supreme contempt, building shabby "camps" as temporary shelters for its laborers, then abandoning them when the work moves on to fresh valleys. The camps of the future will be "trailer courts" inhabited by diminishing numbers of people whose companions will be drilling rigs, bulldozers, power shovels, and coal augers.

Already a million acres of Appalachia have been blasted and bulldozed into ruin. Already 10,700 miles of streams have been severely damaged, half of which have been destroyed past any present hope of restoration. On their way to the sea Appalachia's streams now carry a horrendous freight of silt from murdered mountains, sulfuric acid from unsealed mines, untreated human and animal wastes, and practically every other imaginable form of filth, trash, and litter. As extraction speeds up, new contaminants of many kinds are certain to befoul them, to become permanent additives to much of the nation's drinking water.

The institutions that destroy Appalachia will include every major steel corporation and, as always in enterprises of pollution and ruin, the great names in petroleum. Enormous sums will flow in from Japan and western Europe to finance new wells, mines, and railway spurs. On some days thousands of railroad cars of Appalachian minerals will wait to unload at Hampton Roads, Virginia. Out of this dying land new multitudes of people will swarm in their ancient cars, headed for the slums of every city where rumor has it that jobs can be found. They will carry with them the tenacious Appalachian culture that Arnold Toynbee believes to constitute a dire internal threat to Western civilization. These "hillbillies" will bedevil mayors and city planners whose institutions are already smothering beneath previous waves of unassimilated people.

No state will deal effectively with any of these problems. Governors, judges, and legislators elected with funds supplied by the extractive industries will condone and legalize the spreading destruction and depopulation. The Congress will ignore the abysmal situation except for occasional increases in welfare appropriations and the

---

[OVERLEAF]

". . . in that forever irretrievable moment when wilderness began at the Blue Ridge, the American naturalist was luckier than he is today. Now he has everything he could wish for, except the virginity of his love. No one man can call the Shenandoah his own. And there is left no longer any beyond. You could think once how beyond the Blue Ridge rose the Great Smokies, and beyond them in turn green Tennessee, unknown Kentucky, unbroken forests of beech trees larger than Saxony, Navarre, Galicia. To the civilization at the mouth of the Mississippi, there floated down logs of sycamore and gum and cypress that told of an unexplored world of giants to the north. There were true tales of caverns where the fish and beetles had no eyes for eternal darkness, pine-ringed lakes where the swans were drifted like the snow, and one great meadow like the empire of the Tsar where a wild cattle snuffed the flowers and stamped until the earth shook."

—*Donald Culross Peattie* (Green Laurels)

building of a few expensive and generally ineffective flood-control impoundments.

The generation of concerned young Americans now coming to adulthood will discover this desecration and will loudly protest it. But their protests while heard will produce little change. Since the year 1000 the discovery of immense new stores of resources coupled with endless technological innovations have elevated living standards enormously, but society is still essentially feudal, still fundamentally composed of barons and serfs. The distinction is one of power. The industrialists—that is the destroyers and polluters—are the barons. They sit in boardrooms where the weight of limitless millions focuses. The serfs are the millions of one-vote citizens whose taxes subsidize and support the system. They can never reach the ear of a president or governor, and their usual, and usually worthless, way of asserting an opinion or preference is a letter to the editor. As was the case in feudal England, the barons blithely disregard them while acquiring new tax immunities, new special privileges, and new millions.

An observer writing in the British *Manchester Guardian* for March 7, 1970, noted that the power of huge international corporations is growing to exceed that of the nation-states, raising grave questions about the capacity of government to control them. Certainly there is small likelihood that they will be checked in the primitive backlands of Appalachia. And as the land declines

people from east, west, north and south will make their way to the little enclaves of preserved beauty—the Great Smoky Mountains National Park, the ribbons of still verdant land in the national forests, and the tiny but lovely state parks. To get to them visitors will traverse a nightmare of devastation. Once arrived, their sewage, their trash and litter, their exhaust fumes and noise, indeed their very numbers, will choke and overwhelm those small territories reserved for their pleasure. Thus all alike will be lost.

As they survey the bedraggled remnants, men may be moved to murmur with Whittier, "Of all sad words of tongue or pen, the saddest are these: 'It might have been.'"

When the first puny man stood erect and realized within the hazy depths of his little brain that he was different, he grasped a club or stone for a weapon and stared straight into the snarling face of some huge and hungry predator. He had only a fighting chance to survive and carry his genes down to a later time. He took the chance and fought and won. He has won at every great crisis in his racial history, though it has often been a very close-run thing. Now when he faces the threat of self-extermination from overpopulation, pollution, and the devastation of his planet, he retains, at best, only a fighting chance. His protoplasm must change and adapt, or perish.

If they care to make the fight, Americans have a slender chance to preserve the remaining splendor, beauty, and riches of Appalachia in a state of perpetual usefulness as the habitation of millions and an inspiration for all.

Once again Eliot Porter, America's master photographer, has shown us the indescribable natural beauty of our continent. The emphasis here is on the Smokies, jewel of the Appalachians, and the country's most visited park. Yet what we see is merely a remnant of our matchless mountain heritage. Our ability to protect this remnant—and others like it—will reveal the quality of our civilization as we approach the twenty-first century.

"We travel together, passengers on a little space ship, dependent on its vulnerable reserves of air and soil; all committed for our safety to its security and peace; preserved from annihilation only by the care, the work, and, I will say, the love we give our fragile craft."

—Adlai Stevenson